D1242276

THE POWER'S INSIDE

A TRANSFORMATIONAL GUIDBOOK ON
HOW TO MAXIMIZE YOUR POTENTIAL
and UNLEASH YOUR GREATNESS!

JEFFREY ANTHONY MILLER

Acknowledgements

For Marilyn and Steffani and Maggie

Thank you for your non-stop love and support and for giving me my heart and hope and joy.

And to Dr. Curtis L. Ivery

A giant of a man; leader, educator, my mentor and friend. Thank you for believing in me and for making it happen for *us*.

print ISBN: 978-1-09839-977-1

ebook ISBN: 978-1-09839-978-8

CONTENTS

THE POWER'S INSIDE
AUTHOR'S NOTE

No doubt you've heard the saying somewhere along your journey. The phrase is prominent in the song 'Looking for Love', which featured the lyric hook: *looking for love in all the wrong places, looking for love in too many faces, searching their eyes looking for traces of what I'm dreaming of.*

That refrain kept up a resounding repeat in my brain as I thought how best to begin this work, 'The Power's Inside', and what hook *I* would use to engage those I hoped would read it.

And though I'm not certain where the decades long debate stands between philosophers and sociologists as to whether love or power is the most compelling human desire, I am pretty darn sure that they're each at the top of most people's wish list when it comes to dream fulfillment and personal satisfaction.

Love and power have a lot in common. They're both instigators of change and upheaval, both the essence of human need and human conflict. They're both elusive to many and each is extremely fragile and simultaneously, quite hard to hold onto. Love and power are valuable currencies that rivals try to steal, or scoundrels seek to disrupt. They share another characteristic as well. Only a small percentage of the almost eight billion individuals that share our world will ever taste the full flavor or savor the sweetness of either one.

Like the misguided lover described in the song, who constantly picked the wrong type, the wrong venue, or the wrong location to find the soulmate that would provide happiness and help him get through the night, most who seek the power to direct their fate, to help them find respect, success and a rewarding life are also looking in all the wrong places.

Some people look in the pill bottle, the gym or the workplace for their power. Some plumb the investment and money markets trying to find theirs. Others turn to individuals, or groups and institutions perceived to have power, hoping that some of it will rub off on them. A few, resort to violence against the weak or crimes targeting the vulnerable in their quest to acquire power and adopt a mindset of "the end justifies the means" to rationalize their actions.

The unfortunate fact for most of the folks I just described is that the majority of them will fail in their attempt to secure personal power. Several may get lucky, and a few may be fortunate to have a financially comfortable life, but the power to *control their own destiny* will not be in their hands. Other people with different agendas will dictate their opportunities.

Consequently, for people who look in all these places for personal power, there will always be a void; always a sense of something missing. There will never be enough magic pills in the bottle, never enough weights at the gym, never enough satisfaction or growth on the job, never enough money or possessions to provide lifelong contentment and peace of mind.

True power is having the ability to change things. Change yourself, change your situation, change your circumstances and change your world. True power derives from *maximized individual potential* and is generated from inside you. The power is inside you right now. That is the only place to find it. This book will help you locate your power and show you how to activate it to propel you to the place of your dreams.

Jeffrey Miller

CHAPTER ONE

IT'S SURVIVAL OF THE FITTEST IN A POST COVID-19 WORLD

History has shown that when a civilization changes direction, it is often because of a phenomenon known as a critical juncture. Something so significant occurred, something so disastrous or momentous happened, that society would be forever altered through the decisions made by those who sought to maintain the existing order of things, and the actions taken by those who fought to establish a new course.

The fall of the Roman Empire. The Black Plague. The Black Death in the 1300's that wiped out sixty percent of Europe's population. The arrival of Christopher Columbus. Opening the Atlantic Ocean to triangular trade. The American Revolution. Lewis & Clark's expedition to map the United States. The Russian Revolution & Communism. The world-wide shift from monarchies to pluralistic governments, and the U.S. Civil War are just a few past critical junctures that shaped the way we now live and think.

And though I can't be sure how this COVID-19 pandemic will play out, I can say with certainty that this *is* one of those critical junctures, especially if you like me are trying to live your purpose. What *you* do next, will determine your fate. What we choose to do together *now* will form the future. What we improve today will make it better for our children and theirs.

The years 2020 and 2021 will go down in the books as a major critical juncture for the world in general and the USA in particular. Besides the suffering and death, the poverty and homelessness, the hunger and loss, the fear and divisiveness millions of us have experienced in dealing with the coronavirus, millions more were battered, beaten or utterly destroyed by roaring infernos as firenados burned California, while record setting forest fires devoured much of the rest of the American West.

They were over-run by torrential rains and historic floods as hurricane after hurricane after hurricane engulfed our coastal areas, and devastated by economic drought as industries and businesses, services and churches, cities, states and towns shut down, cancelled, furloughed, shuttered, or curtailed life as we knew it, before COVID-19 emerged.

This "new day", this post COVID-19 "re-birth", has us grappling with uncertainty, apprehension and erosion. Trust in our political process has been eroded due to non-stop lies and distortion, cronyism and toadyism, incompetence and immorality and action based on partisanship or political affiliation.

Trust in our information process, our traditional media establishment, has been eroded by social media platforms, unsubstantiated posts, personal newsfeeds, manipulative misinformation and political bias.

Trust in our society's cohesive institutions, the glue that holds us all together: Law Enforcement, the Judicial System, National Security, the Scientific Community, the Medical System, the Postal Service, and even the integrity of our Election Process, has also been eroded.

As if all this isn't enough to make us want to holler (or hide) this massive erosion has uncovered many of the pathologies most of us thought we had buried deep. Open police brutality and blatant racism. Conspiracy theories. Inequality and discrimination based on age, ethnicity, finance or immigrant status. A sordid national history. White supremacy, Black rage, sub-standard wages, and far too many of us hanging on by our fingernails and worried that we are losing our chance.

The new day ushered in by the coronavirus brings with it a new reality. Not only are we still dealing with its ravages, but we're also bleeding red ink. The U.S. Federal deficit for 2020 was more than three trillion dollars, approximately 18% of our projected GDP, which is the largest annual deficit the United States has experienced since 1945. For comparison, the deficit in 2019 was 984 billion dollars or just 5% of GDP. GDP stands for Gross Domestic Product and is the total value of goods and services produced in a country. Big deficits mean a growing Federal debt which also means that our country is paying a ton of interest to service this debt.

Point of fact, the U.S. Government spent as much on interest in 2020 than on the *combined* annual budgets of the departments of Commerce, Education, Energy, Homeland Security, Housing and Urban Development, and the Interior, Justice and State Departments!

Just about every state in the Union was pleading with the Feds to send them big money to help them pay the bills. Business shutdowns and lack of consumer spending resulted in state tax revenue being way down. Major financial shortfalls were projected and cuts to services, social and otherwise, were expected.

Unemployment was sky high, rivaling numbers we hadn't seen since the Great Depression. Whole industries: restaurants, retail, malls, movie theatres, casinos, travel, hotels, airlines and cruise ships remain in deep financial trouble. Hundreds of thousands were terminated or laid off. With all this loss, fear and anxiety are so prevalent that the mental health services are on overload.

Change was everywhere. Work from home if you were lucky. Office parks and high rise office complexes were closed or at limited capacity. Women left the workforce in droves. School lessons were delivered by Zoom and Microsoft Teams. Parents doubled as classroom teachers. Many students were left out because the digital divide is real and deep.

Food banks couldn't keep up with the demand. The population was divided between the haves and the have nots. The haves: those who could work from home and didn't live paycheck to paycheck. The have nots: those who lost their job, or couldn't work from home, or did live paycheck to paycheck and put their lives on the line as "essential workers" to keep that paycheck coming. Shopping online. Curbside pickup. Touchless contact. Shortage of coins. Business meetings through WebEx. Food delivered to your door. See the doctor on-line. Are you ready for this? Are you ready for what's coming in this post COVID-19 world?

If not, then I suggest you quickly get ready because the health of our nation; its physical health, its financial health and even (as evidenced by the apprehension and dread as to what would be the outcome of the 2020 Presidential election) its mental health is not at all good.

Ready or not a new day has dawned and to my mind, this new day, this post COVID-19 day demands an entirely new way. Especially since the old ways, the pre-COVID safety nets, the pre-COVID expectations, the pre-COVID attitudes, the pre-COVID structure no longer holds.

It appears to my wide-open eyes that for at least the next decade, maybe more, *survival of the fittest* will be the new reality. In this post COVID-19 era, it may not be every man or woman for him or herself, but as we dig ourselves out of the holes fighting this virus has created, and erect new foundations, nobody is going to make it fair for you but you. Nobody is going to get your fair share for you but you. So, what do you do now?

To have any chance of getting your fair share in this critical juncture time, you've got to know and use the power inside you, your personal power, your physical and mental power and ultimately, the enormous power of your potential.

CHAPTER TWO

FOUR ELEMENTS TO MAX-YO-PO

To maximize your potential, that's the name of the game, that's the key. Maximized potential is knowing how to use all that God gave you to become everything you're capable of being. To use your intellect, your massive brain power. To use your humanity, your knowledge, your physical strength, your endurance and all five of your senses. To use your perception and persistence, your talent and brilliance, your warmth and compassion, your humor and empathy. To tap into your drive and determination, unburdened by self-doubt or fear of failure.

Maximized potential is your total package, firing on all cylinders to produce the outcome you desire. Potential refers to all that you are, but maximized potential is about all that you can *become,* your greatness!

To reach your potential, I've identified twelve essential components which I call the Empowerment Principles. These principles form the basis of the Empowerment Project curriculum I created and have taught for the past thirteen years. Personal Empowerment leads to Self-Actualization because Personal Empowerment provides the road-map to follow to *Max-Yo-Po*, to maximize your individual potential.

To Max-Yo-Po, four distinct elements have to work in harmony, and they have to mesh like gears to provide your momentum. The elements are *Mindset, Behavior, Action Steps* and *Individual Planning.* Each one is essential to the Max-Yo-Po process, and each must work in sync with the others.

But of all the four elements, **Mindset** may be the most critical because it is your Mindset that drives your behavior. Your Mindset creates your desire to act. It's your Mindset that develops the content for your individual plan and determines the success or failure of that plan. Your Mindset is the fuel that generates the power that will drive you to your destiny.

Now I'm not talking about your personal opinion on a subject or what you may believe in when I use the word Mindset, I'm talking about something much, much bigger. Your Mindset is how you approach the world and is shaped in part by how the world responds to your approach.

A Mindset that is receptive to new ideas, prospects, diverse people or different places, in other words that is optimistic and actively engaged in meeting life head on, opens doors and provides opportunity because of the positivity that Mindset radiates.

On the other hand, a Mindset that is closed due to cynicism or indifference; bad prior experiences; a lack of confidence; fear or prejudice; or a know it all, "been there done that" attitude will not only shut off opportunity, but it will also produce behavior that blocks momentum because a Mindset that is closed or negative results in minimal action. The way we think controls what we do so it is our Mindset that drives our behavior.

Behavior is one of those words that conjures up a sense of unease in people who hear the word directed toward them. I think because often the word behavior is used to indicate someone's negative or corrective response to either our actions or inaction. I can't count the number of times in my life that my mother or some teacher, coach or other authority figure told me that if I didn't modify my behavior, I'd be in some kind of trouble.

The word always put me on the defensive, which made me uptight and tense because it seemed that those who told me that were finding fault with me, doubting my intentions or trying to control me in some way. The relevant fact about the word behavior though is that the synonym for this big, intimidating three syllable word is a teeny-tiny one syllable word with great big impact: *DO*.

Behavior is simply what you do, and it is what you do or don't do that establishes the level of success that you will attain in this life. Mindset determines what we do. Mindset influences what we don't do. Mindset affects how we do it. Mindset is an attitude and as you may already know, a positive mental attitude produces maximum altitude, with it you'll rise high.

Do is an action word. In this post COVID-19 world, this survival of the fittest existence you've got to do daily, you've got to do now. You've got to do tomorrow and the day after that! You can't wait for somebody else to bring it or give it. They may, but when everybody is struggling to make it through, if you're not able to do for yourself and those who count on *you* to make it, chances are better than 50-50 that you *won't* make it.

Action Steps, the third essential element necessary to Max-Yo-Po, is where the rubber of your Mindset meets the road of your Behavior. Since behavior's synonym 'do' is an action word this element is where you actively set yourself up to win!

Choices, desires, habits and impulses can all be realized through action, but it is your Mindset that decides what action to take. Actions that keep your options open. Actions that don't cause you or yours physical or mental harm. Actions that lay the foundation for the next leg of your journey. Actions that allow you to see yourself moving forward and making progress. Actions that don't take you out of the game.

Simply put, a closed Mindset will not result in any of that and will probably produce actions that result in stagnation, but an open Mindset, with a positive, can-do attitude brings about personal growth. Personal growth, combined with careful planning will help you prepare for the survival of the fittest world left in the wake of COVID-19, the Monster of Dread.

Notice I said careful planning. Your **individual plan,** the fourth essential element to Max-Yo-Po will provide the blueprint, the GPS and the "how-to" guide to follow in your quest to reach that place called success.

But here's the thing about a plan, for a plan to succeed it must be written down. A plan that is not written down, that is just floating around in your mind is only an idea; an idea that will be pushed out of your head or moved to the back of your consciousness when the next big idea comes to mind.

A plan, a written document to refer to, revise, and use to chart your progress becomes a step by step manual on how to achieve the objective you have set. Your plan tells you what you need to do to drive your action. Your plan, crafted and decided on by you. A plan born of your **Mindset,** made possible by your **Behavior** and driven by the **Actions** you take to get it done.

Need a car, a new house, an apartment or additional education? You need a plan. Late on the rent, the mortgage or the utilities? You need a plan to get out from behind the eight ball. Caring for elderly relatives, a house-full of extended family and/or school age children? You need a plan to make it all work. Want to launch a new career, need to find a life partner or spouse, desire to start a business or move to a different city? You need a plan. Determined to get out of an abusive situation or find a better paying job? You need a plan for that too.

For my Empowerment Project curriculum, I developed a lesson plan that defines and outlines the individual planning process. Since 2008, I've taught my program to hundreds of students from high school age to middle age and most points in between.

I've taught for government agencies, training academies, a community college, and non-profit associations. I've given seminars at churches, high schools, neighborhood block clubs and wherever else I've been invited. And I kid you not; no one, not one of my students had ever written an action plan and most had no idea how to start one let alone drive one!

Remember, to maximize your potential all four elements must be working in perfect harmony, meshing seamlessly; not one element or two but all four; *Mindset, Behavior, Action Steps* and *Individual Planning*. Combined they provide all the fuel you'll need to boost you to your next level.

Without a proper plan however, a plan to guide your action, you're missing a crucial gear, an essential element, and you're hindering your ability to apply the personal power that maximized potential provides.

It's about to get really tight in this country as we prepare to brave the chaotic period made worse by the capricious and deadly coronavirus. Political turmoil threatens our peace of mind, and the economic recovery is uncertain. News reports are rampant with the discord and divide among our population. A sizeable percentage of U.S citizens refuses to acknowledge the reality of the contagion spread, not just by COVID-19 but also the toxic social climate that propagates, anger, fear, lies and violence. Guns and bullets are again jumping from the store shelves. Domestic terrorism and ethnic hatred are on the rise.

To thrive, not just survive will take all that you've got, all the power of your vast potential. This book, *'The Power's Inside'* will help you Max-Yo-Po by providing two things:

- The Guide to **Personal Empowerment**: "The Knowledge and Ability to Remove or Overcome *Any* Obstacle or Impediment that Blocks the Acquisition of Individual Achievement".

- The Blueprint to follow to **Self-Actualization**: "Acquiring the Drive, Determination, Motivation and Skill-Set to Realize Your Full Potential Through Action"!

CHAPTER THREE

THE FOUR THINGS ALMOST EVERYBODY ON THE PLANET IS TRYING TO DO

On the landmass of the planet Earth approximately eight billion human beings reside. They live diverse lives on the seven continents and numerous islands, surrounded, bordered or dissected by the seas and rivers that encompass seventy one percent of our globe.

The earthlings speak different languages, follow different customs, appear in different colors and different sizes; embrace different spiritual beliefs, engage in different rituals, come from different cultures, and adopt different ideas.

Because of all this difference, students often react to my assertion made on the first day of class that the vast majority of these world citizens all want to do the *exact same* four things, with bewilderment, skepticism or disbelief; until that is, I break it down.

"Raise your hand if you agree with this statement," I ask. "The majority of Africans, Asians, Australians, Europeans, North Americans, South Americans and people that work in Antarctica; no matter their gender, political agenda, education level, income or sexual orientation *all* want to do *exactly* the same four things that each of you sitting in this classroom wants to do."

Puzzled expressions respond to my declaration, but no hands raise. "What if I told you," I continued "that each of you taking this Course wants to do the exact same four things that every other student in this room or even on this planet is trying to do, would you agree with me?" Quizzical looks and negative headshakes provide my answer.

Moving to the dry erase whiteboard and beginning to write under the heading: FOUR THINGS JUST ABOUT EVERYBODY ON THE PLANET IS TRYING TO DO: I begin to make my point.

"Almost every one of the eight billion people who share this world with you want to OBTAIN, MAINTAIN, SUSTAIN AND ATTAIN." Turning back to the class and attempting to start the student-teacher give and take that is so critical to establishing rapport, connecting with my cohort and involving them in the learning process, I prod with a smile, "ok, somebody give me a three letter word that is a synonym for the word obtain."

'Get', someone calls out. Nodding affirmatively, I say, "somebody give us a four letter word that means the same thing as maintain." A couple of hands shoot up but before I can call on someone, a voice from the back blurts out, '*keep*'. "How about a four letter word that means the same as sustain," I ask. Met by silence, I try another couple questions. "Do we have any urban farmers in the room? What does it mean to sustain a crop? Do we have any parents in the room? What does it mean to sustain a family?"

I wait a few seconds for the answer. No hands raise, but from the corner a lady with a questioning tone says '*grow*'? "Exactly" I nod, beaming at her, happy that they're getting into it. "All right" I continue, "who wants to give us the synonym for attain?" No one answers at first, so I provide a few hints.

"What does it mean to attain a degree that you've worked hard for, or attain a place on the team you've always wanted to play for? What does it mean to attain your dream career? What does it mean to attain the house you've saved years to buy, or attain a pay raise for the job that your superior work earned"? Hands shoot up! I gesture, pointing to them all. 'To *succeed*' they say in unison. All right I think, now it's coming into focus. To clarify my point, I move into lecture mode.

"Unless they are very young or extremely old, just about everybody living on this planet wants to do the same four things that everybody else wants to do. We all want to get the things we need and want. We all want to keep the things we get. We all want to grow the things we've been able to keep and ultimately we all want to succeed throughout every step of our life's journey.

We don't want to do just one of these things or two of them; we want to do all four! What good is it to get the things we need or want and not be able to keep them? How satisfying is it to keep the things we've been able to get, but not be able to grow our opportunities to acquire more? And if we human beings are unable to *get* or *keep* or *grow* the things we need and want then there's no way to *succeed*.

Therein lies the worldwide dissatisfaction, disillusionment and despair. The cause of the endless wars, constant coups and ethnic atrocities.

This is what triggers the hopelessness of the world's refugees who can't do any of the four things. This is what makes American inner cities wither and rural areas stagnate. This is what provokes the protests and the riots and the terrorists. This is what produces the autocratic leadership that lifts one group of people at the expense of another.

This desire: this need to obtain, maintain, sustain and attain is the driver of both human advancement and human turmoil. It is the creator of hope and hopelessness, joy and misery."

Dropping the lecture mode and adopting an inquisitive tone I throw it back to the class. "Why do you think there are so many people throughout the world that are unable to do all four of these things?"

Their answers come fast and furious. "There's too many people on the planet and not enough to go around," says one. "It's racism," says a guy in the front. "No, it's sexism," says a lady in the corner. "That's not it," chimes a strong voice from the middle of the cohort. "It's that a fraction of the people on the globe own all the wealth, and they don't want to let the other people (the majority of the people) have anything."

The room was bubbling. We'd only been together for a few minutes, but I could tell this was going to be a receptive and engaged group. I stood silent for a while to let them settle down. After the last comment I asked, "remember your elementary school English classes? What kind of words are get, keep, grow and succeed?" 'Verbs', someone responds.

"Exactly" I reply enthusiastically, "they're verbs, they're *action* words. You've got to *do* something to get what you need and want. You've got to do even more to be able to keep what you've been able to get. You've got to do repeatedly, continuously and consistently to grow what you've been able to keep; and you've got to do it over and over and over again to succeed, not just for today but for all your tomorrows." A hand goes up. "Why do you think so many people can't do these four things Mr. Miller," a young lady asks.

To speak to that question, let me step out of the classroom and talk to you directly. The easy answer is that most people just don't know how to do it, or even what they're trying to do, which is one of the reasons I wrote this book. It's deeper and more complex though than not knowing the how or the what; you've also got to know the who, where, when and the why to accomplish each of 'The Four Things', which is why I teach Personal Empowerment.

Without a doubt there are tremendous external forces in play that block a person's ability to accomplish any one of these things let alone all four.

Societal forces like authoritarian government regimes that dole out opportunity like party favors to the well connected. Forces like systemic racism that excludes people from participation in a misguided effort to control or contain them. Forces like wealth inequity, that relegates most of the world's people to inferior living conditions, concentrated poverty, sub-standard education and ignorance of not just what is possible to obtain, but ignorant also of the means to change their condition.

The hard answer to the young lady's question is perhaps the most destructive force of all. The persistent (some say deliberate) dumbing down of the population while instilling in us the erroneous belief that we each *deserve* to have it all and if we don't then it's somebody else's fault.

In essence, the four things most everybody on the planet is trying to do provides the contour of human existence on this earth. It takes hard work, performed ably and consistently over the entirety of our life's journey, to obtain, maintain, sustain and attain, so some people cheat to get what they need or try to take what someone else is trying to keep. Some folks are lazy or unmotivated. A lot of us lack confidence. Some get stuck on the obtaining part. Others can't get past the maintaining. Many try to skip the work and go straight to the attain through deceit, scam fueled lies, and manipulative actions.

With billions of people walking among us all trying to do the exact same four things you're trying to do you'll need an advantage to get your share and you'll need to compete. When you compete, you'll need to win more than you lose which is why it's essential to Max-Yo-Po. Maximizing your potential begins with Personal Empowerment because to be empowered means *to know.*

CHAPTER FOUR

TO BE EMPOWERED MEANS

In the last 25 years our society has undergone a massive shift in direction as we've moved (at Mach 10 speed) into the Digital and Technological Age. This "Techno-Revolution", ushered in at the dawn of the 21st century, has altered our world in ways every bit as shattering as the Industrial Revolution a century ago changed the world for our ancestors, just a couple generations removed.

In the 21st century its brains over brawn now, mind over matter. NAFTA, the North American Free Trade Agreement forged under Bush and Clinton in the mid 1990's, (and replaced in 2016 with the US-Mexico-Canada Agreement by Trump) has forever changed where the goods we buy are made.

It's also resulted in closed factories, bankrupt plants, failed businesses, downsized companies and a trade imbalance with China. NAFTA served as the instigator of change as our nation morphed from a manufacturing-based economy into a service based economic model.

Bottom line is we no longer make much of what we need, we import it. Which means that the jobs and the money and the opportunity to earn a good living have been *exported*; shipped off to another country or continent while many of us struggle *here* to adapt and make the transition to the "new order of things": Digital, Software, Robots, Devices, Instant Communication by Satellite Transmission and Cyber Hack Attacks.

Over the past two and a half decades we've experienced and been made to embrace a new, vastly different level of competition. Now we compete not just against each other for opportunity, but also against technology in the quest to obtain, maintain, sustain and attain.

The so-called "service-based economy" may have, as people thought in the 1990's, been enough to sustain America's workforce but back then most didn't see the drastic change coming.

They didn't foresee that the "Techno-Revolution" would knock the human worker right out of the box, or that whole industries would be decimated by the shift to digital. Many were slow to grasp that a new way of doing *everything* would spring up and that the jobs they thought we'd now have would be taken by innovative software programs, robots that multi-task and devices that never call in sick, don't demand benefits, and never expect a pension or a raise.

The fact is, the ideas embedded during the Industrial Revolution; work long, hard hours and prosper, innovate and succeed, have been altered a century later by the Digital Revolution's reality. It's no longer just about hard work and a willingness to put in the hours. Now you've got to outdo the competition to succeed.

To win today we've got to be better; better than the machines and better equipped to ride the waves of change. Now more than ever before we need an edge to get over the top. In the 21st century, that edge comes from being *Empowered*.

Empowerment is one of those words that means different things to whomever hears it or says it, which also means that it's a word that is often ignored or misunderstood.

"We need to empower the Women," say those who believe the female gender has not been given equal opportunity or respect. "We've got to empower the Blacks," say those that know African Americans have been denigrated, discriminated against and excluded.

"We need to empower the LGBTQ community," say advocates who've faced hatred and rejection. "We need to empower Hispanics and Latinos," advise people that advocate for ethnic inclusion and equality.

Some even say that 'The Church' needs to be empowered, while others admonish that we must empower 'The Youth" to do the right thing. But what does that mean exactly? How do you empower a group?

One of the attributes of power is its ability to change something or to stop something from being changed. Societal power is either about rearranging and/or replacing *those who would keep things as they are* (the status quo), or in the case of the status quo, trying to maintain the existing order of things.

Societal power is a continuous struggle between those who would supersede the status quo or alter their policies, and those intent on resisting change by any means necessary, in an effort to hold on to power. Societal power ultimately is about control of the people, the infrastructure, the economics and the future.

Full disclosure when it comes to personal empowerment I'm all in for "power to the people". In fact, I've been teaching and living that doctrine for most of my adult life, but here's the thing. Every time I hear a spokesperson for some marginalized group of American citizens say that "we need to empower"... I always wonder which *"we"* they're talking about.

Is our system of bureaucratic government, social service fairness agencies, and partisan politicians that offer self-seeking elective leadership the *"we"* these advocates beseech for power? Is it the K-12 education apparatus, the community colleges, the universities, the jobs training programs and apprenticeships that should provide the empowerment the change agents demand?

Is the "*we*" the 'Private Sector': the employers, business owners, managers, diversity officials, human resource executives, and union stewards? Perhaps it's the Money People. The brokers, and bankers, the capitalists, investors and hedge fund managers that these protestors seek to link with to drive the change they desire.

Could the "*we*" be the Techno Billionaires? Perhaps they might combine their clout with the dollars earned from the information, entertainment, advertising and promotional companies to whom they sell our data. Maybe these Billionaires could join forces with their corporate clients to provide the "power of the purse" to foment the change the people hope to see.

I think you get where I'm going here. "*We need to empower*" as a rallying cry or a call to action is a fallacy, a false notion, because none of our societal pillars, with the possible exception of our education apparatus is in place to change the structure of our systems. They were *erected by* the status quo! The pillars are there to support the structures, to keep them standing strong and to maintain the existing order of things.

To call on these societal pillars for help in empowering people, marginalized or otherwise, goes against the reason the structures they support were erected in the first place. It's as if a rabbit calls out for the fox to save it from the coyote; success is not a possible outcome for the rabbit.

To change your circumstance, improve your situation, realize your purpose, and live your life to its fullest does take maximized power, but it won't be generated by external forces. The power to change things for you, and those who depend on you is an *internal* force; that power is already *inside* you.

To activate your personal power is not that complex. All you have to do is acknowledge and recognize its presence, understand its force, learn how to develop it, and discover how best to use it. That process starts with *Personal Empowerment*.

To be empowered means a whole lot of things but most of all it means to *know*. To know more than those who would keep you down or out of the game know. It means to be *"Super-Literate"*, comfortable and at ease with not only the language, but also with finance and technology.

To be empowered means to know where you're coming from *and* to know where you're headed. It means keeping your options open to provide multiple choices. It means knowing how to handle yourself, how to act, in *all* situations. It means knowing how to communicate to get what you need *and* to resolve conflict effectively. It also means not having to look over your shoulder because somebody might be coming for you.

To be empowered means cleaning up tickets, paying off debts or past due financial obligations so that one can operate unencumbered and maneuver freely. It means not being fearful and it means being able to give to others.

In addition, it means having the ability to *SELF-ACTUALIZE*; to know, like you know your own name, *all* that you can become. To be empowered means to fully understand and apply what you know to ignite your greatness (Max-Yo-Po) by acquiring the drive, determination, motivation and skill-set to realize your full potential through action!

When we're young, most of us fantasize of doing big, important and impactful things when we grow up. If we're lucky in childhood, we've been motivated to reach for our dreams by the deeds of inventors and builders, innovators and risk takers. If we were really fortunate in our youth, we were inspired by writers and poets, singers and speakers to shoot for the stars.

Once grown, many of these daydreams and big ideas fade into the recess of memory as most people are consumed by trying to do the four things almost everybody else is trying to do. The daily grind and effort, the uncertainty and repetitiveness of obtaining, maintaining, sustaining and attaining move to the forefront of our mind and becomes the focus of our consciousness. Thoughts of internal greatness recede even further.

The unfortunate by-product of this *mindset* of acquisition and the *behavior* it produces when the result is insufficient, is a self-defeating attitude of rationalization. A sort of "settling" becomes the main method of dealing with the frustration of not being able to get, keep, grow or succeed on a consistent basis.

"That's good enough" becomes a trusted mantra. "I've got more than my neighbors" is a comforting fallback position. Thoughts of "my property is bigger than his", or "my house is nicer than hers", serve as a buffer to personal failure and act as a magic potion that makes settling for a mundane, unfulfilling or uneventful life easier to swallow.

This mindset of "settling" is what blocks *Self-Actualization*. These "that's good enough", "I've got more than some", "mine is better than yours" coping mechanisms that so many of us use actually stops Self-Actualization like Kevlar stops a bullet.

Why? Because the mindset and behavior of Self-Actualization is not about the other person, it's about you. Self-Actualization isn't about comparing yourself to me or my accomplishments, it's about developing you into your own greatness.

Self-Actualization is all about **self**. Not stopping your**self** until you reach the place manifested in your dreams. Not settling for doing the things everybody else is trying to do, or settling even further, as you bounce like a pinball from the flipper to a bumper then deep in the hole.

Since the beginning of recorded time, despite the gravitational pull exerted by 'The Four Things', high achievers in every culture have managed to achieve Self-Actualized status. What they've used to avoid the mental trap of "that's good enough" and what makes them seemingly immune to the "settling" rationalization involves another concept of **self**, confidence.

Self-confidence is the bridge that connects Personal Empowerment to Self-Actualization. Self-confidence is that rare blend of awareness, capability and experience that is the essential component to being able to turn on your power at will. Confidence in your ability and your character that is born, nourished, reinforced, sustained and cemented from knowing, not just who you are, but what you're about.

Self-confidence is derived from past actions performed successfully. Confidence that grows from knowing how to communicate with virtually anyone to have your viewpoint considered and your ideas and input respected. Confidence that you can handle through knowledge and experience any difficulty you encounter or meet any challenge that comes your way. Confidence that you can discern the difference between a lie and the truth, or what is real versus fake.

Self-confidence is what allows Self-Actualized people to try again and again and again, because they know that success and failure are but two different sides of the very same coin. Through the course of my journey, I've identified twelve confidence builders that I call *'The Empowerment Principles'*. These principles lead to Self-Actualization, which is why I refer to Personal Empowerment as the bridge.

The Principles:

1. Super-Literacy Is Job #1

2. Knowing Where You Came From

3. Knowing Where You're Headed

4. Knowing How To Handle Yourself

5. Knowing How To Communicate

6. Having Options And Choices

7. Not Being Fearful

8. Not Being Victimized

9. Not Looking Over Your Shoulder

10. Cleaning Up Tickets, Debts & Financial Obligations

11. Being Able To Give To Others

12. Being Able To Turn On Your Own Ignition

Each one of these principles can be used as solid planks in the bridge you build to cross into the Maximized Potential realm. In laying these planks, you'll be able to absorb their power to support you. They'll also generate the fuel to drive momentum and the energy to lift you to Self-Actualization.

Once there, you'll be equipped with all that you need to win much more often than you lose. You'll possess the knowledge of self and the confidence to pursue your goals secure in your ability to direct your own course, control your own destiny, live your purpose and meet whatever comes head on.

CHAPTER FIVE

THE ROAD TO EMPOWERMENT BEGINS AT CURIOSITY'S DOOR

Curiosity is the gateway to Personal Empowerment. From the moment I became aware of the connection between the two, I've questioned why so many of us either can't see the gateway or deliberately try to keep the gateway closed.

Not long ago I was standing in a socially distanced check-out line at a 'we sell everything' big box store. Waiting my turn in the self-service U-Scan line, I couldn't help but notice the interaction between a thirty-something woman unloading a cart full of items in the staffed lane, while the toddler next to her kept up a steady stream of questions.

"What's that mama" she asked, pointing to the credit card reader. "What's that for," the child wanted to know as her mother placed a utensil on the conveyor belt. "Why are you doing that," she asked when her mother took out first her phone, then her coupons. Tugging at her mother's coat while pointing to the impulse items next to the register the little girl cajoled, "Can I get a candy bar?"

The woman ignored the chatter and didn't answer any of her daughter's questions, just continued unloading her things and making small talk with the cashier. Meanwhile, the wide-eyed kid kept the barrage of questions coming.

"Did you get the Cocoa Puffs"? "Why is that man pushing all those carts"? "Where are we going after this; do I have to take a nap when we get home"? Pointing to a young man without a mask, the precocious youngster said for all to hear, "look at him mama, why doesn't that man have a mask on?"

Her mother, exasperated now, looked down at her child and said sternly, "girl would you shut up! Quit asking so many questions! Can't you see mama's busy"? Uh Oh I said to myself as I saw the little girl's excited eyes dim a bit and watched her expression turn from bright to partly cloudy when her mother shut her down.

For some reason watching this scene reminded me of a high school business development class I recently observed via Zoom. I was a guest speaker, there to talk to the 10th graders about entrepreneurship but I had logged into the session early to get a feel for the students.

One young man in the cohort of approximately twenty pupils repeatedly interrupted the flow of the information with questions. His hand was raised non-stop. I noticed after a few moments that the teacher wasn't calling on this kid almost to the point of ignoring him, so he just started to blurt out his questions (the teacher told me later that he'd kept all the students mikes open because he wanted to encourage a wide range of ideas).

I could see the middle-aged male teacher become increasingly flustered trying to manage the online technology, the lesson plan, twenty students and the inquisitive sophomore's constant disruption. Finally, in a peevish tone the man snapped, "young man, pipe down. Stop interrupting with all your questions or I'll never be able to get through the material planned for today"!

The boy dropped his hand like he'd touched something hot, started to pout and visibly lost interest. That scene also made me think, Uh Oh.

Shaking my head in disapproval of what I'd witnessed in that classroom *and* the store, I finally made it through the U-Scan checkout. Walking to my car through the massive parking lot I thought back on my early jobs and the first days spent trying to figure out what I was supposed to do and how to do it.

My questions to the managers and bosses were often met with responses like, "we'll cover that later" or, "don't have time to go over it right now" or, "you don't need to know that" or, "that's not your department" or "what are you an agitator? Quit rocking the boat with all your questions."

These people held onto information like a prized painting or a stock tip. Some didn't want to share what they knew thinking their knowledge gave them an advantage; still more didn't want to admit that they didn't have the answers and a few, resentful of my being hired, hoped I'd fail.

Considering the way most of us have been raised I shouldn't have been surprised by what I saw in the store or in the classroom. Thinking back on my first jobs, made me think back even further.

When I asked my mother why she said, "because I said so." When I asked my coaches why they answered, "just do it." When I asked the preacher how to believe in something I couldn't see he replied, "just trust me" and when I asked the doctor about his treatment recommendation after reading an opposing idea, the Doc advised, "quit reading so much and listen to me."

As a former broadcast journalist, I know the importance of the 5 W's and the H to telling a complete story. If a writer or reporter, intent on providing maximum detail on a happening or event cannot answer the 5 W's and hopefully the H in their article, audio report or video, they haven't done their job.

When writing a piece, if I can't answer the who, the what, the where, the when, the why and hopefully the how, then I didn't write it right. I've got to answer all the questions because if I don't my reader, who's counting on me to deliver the complete story, won't have all the information. My reader is *curious* and if I'm not equally curious, if I don't care enough or know enough to dig deep to answer all their questions then they can't count on me to deliver, and they won't know.

Above all to be empowered means to know. Without curiosity it is impossible to know much of anything because a non-curious person hasn't learned much of anything, which is why I say, *"The Road to Empowerment Begins at Curiosity's Door."*

To maximize your potential, you've got to pass through curiosity's gate. What you will learn once inside will lead to greater discovery, increased awareness, enhanced capability and expansive options.

A curious person is an *interested* person, an individual that wants to find out things covering all sorts of topics or subjects. A curious person wonders about his or her surroundings, the past and the future, the current possibilities and challenges, unfamiliar places and people, different ideas and new solutions to old problems. They ponder questions like:

Where exactly is heaven? Why don't jet planes fall from the sky? How did they build the Golden Gate and Mackinaw bridges? Is there really a God? How does global warming produce climate change? Why did the smelt disappear from Lake Michigan? Why is it so hard to trust other people? How do you build a mother board? Does might make right? What

was the slave trade? How does the moon affect the tides? Are
Bitcoin and other crypto-currencies safe investments? Why
are there so many different religions in the world?

Curiosity sparks imagination. When something grabs the interest
of a curious person, they want to know more about it. This desire
for more propels them to dig deeper for additional input and search
numerous sources for expanded knowledge. This deeper exploration
into the subject of their interest leads to additional information on
related topics. Their greater awareness and exposure to new insight
boosts self-esteem which helps to stimulate confidence.

This increased confidence engenders the second major benefit of
curiosity. It makes a person *interesting*. Everybody likes a good story.
A storyteller that knows what they're talking about, delivers the tale
with enthusiasm, and is descriptively believable draws a willing and
engaged listener.

If the storyteller can answer the 5 W's and the H and do it with
certainty and confidence in their facts, that listener becomes a crowd;
attracted to the storyteller like honey attracts a bear, drawn to the
storyteller like nectar and pollen draws the bumblebee.

Curiosity initiates the process to maximized potential. In fact,
curiosity is *the* essential component because it helps an individual to
unleash their greatness by discovering their talent(s) and exposing
their brilliance.

Brilliance is one of those words that have two distinct meanings.
On the one hand, to be brilliant means to possess a superior intellect
through the acquisition of considerable knowledge. On the other, to
be brilliant means to emit a bright shining light.

The thing that makes curiosity such an incredibly important
spark to ignite the drive to Personal Empowerment is that it makes

both of these definitions manifest in people. They're more interested so they learn a great deal more than those who aren't curious. They're also more interesting, which allows other people to see their light. Their confidence produces a glow which pulls people to them like a moth, fluttering through a dark summer night, is attracted to a porch light.

Perhaps the most beneficial outcome of a curious mindset is that it allows a person avenues to discover their individual talent(s); their innate, specialized God-given gifts. I'm not talking about a skill, something one becomes good at by repetitive practice over a period of time, when I use the word talent.

I'm talking about something, or a set of somethings, that were born in you when you were born. Things that came here with you, inside you. Gifts that you were equipped with to help you make your way, or your livelihood through this journey of life. Natural things instilled in you by your Creator. God inserted gifts that must be developed for a person to thrive but first must become known.

Unfortunately, many of our fellow travelers, consumed by the demands of trying to accomplish 'The Four Things', don't take or make the time to discover their personalized special gifts. Chasing their needs and wants, searching for the "Good Life", keeping up with the Jones' and trying to hold on, too many folks focus their effort and attention on what's on the outside.

Seldom do they look inside, especially once they've reached adulthood. It becomes easier, then normal to try to emulate or mimic the talents of those we admire than to find our own. It becomes preferable to *"settle"* for a lifestyle that can be earned or supported through their various skills.

But a curious individual, a person that derives stimulation and motivation from finding out about themselves, from needing to learn the answers to life's questions and from seeking to discover, is also a person more likely to *participate* in the things that interest them.

Participation with like-minded people provides a mechanism to compare your attributes to theirs, test yourself against others, try a variety of things and take in new information. This constant comparing, trying, listening, learning and participating will reveal an individual's strengths, likes and focus. Simultaneously, this participatory activity will expose what comes easily to a person; what they can do faster or better than most people, with limited effort or thought; their *talent*!

Participation will also illustrate what areas an individual may struggle in or have difficulty with but can be improved with effort and time. These areas are more likely skill than talent, especially if, when the task is mastered, it's not something that the person particularly enjoys or is excited by.

Knowing this is why I thought Uh Oh as I watched the non-attentive mother and stressed out teacher shut down the inquiring young minds they were supposed to encourage. Uh Oh because this shut down behavior happens to most of us throughout our entire lives but especially when we're young and in our formative stages.

We've all been subjected to comments like: *Curiosity killed the cat. Mind your own business. Do as you're told. Don't go to that neighborhood. What you don't know can't hurt you. That church isn't for you. Watch out for those people, they're different. Why are you reading/watching that? Why were you talking to them?*

Statements, questions and judgements like these are interest discouragers and curiosity killers. They portray a mindset that knowledge of a certain subject or type is unnecessary. They "dumb-down" the population and cause people to *"settle"*.

The empowering traits of curiosity:

- Increased Knowledge through Increased Interest
- Improved Self-Confidence through Increased Knowledge
- Showcased Brilliance: Awareness and Knowledge
- Unleashed Brilliance: Draw People to You
- Discover Your Talent(s)

is why I call it *"The Gateway to Personal Empowerment"*. It's why curiosity should never be discouraged but constantly encouraged, not just when we're young but always because life is a journey not a destination. Empowered people don't *"settle"*. They continue to learn, explore, try and grow well into their 70's and beyond.

In the previous chapter, I talked about using the twelve *Empowerment Principles* as planks in the bridge you build *to Self-Actualization*. Take a minute to review numbers 1, 2 and 3. There's no way to become **Super-Literate, Know Where You're Coming From** or even **Where You're Headed** without curiosity.

CHAPTER SIX

THE ULTIMATE COMPETITIVE ADVANTAGE

One of the dichotomies of the human experience is that we've got to cooperate and work *with* other people to achieve community progress and prosperity, while simultaneously competing *against* them to obtain our individual piece of the good life.

To successfully do the same four things almost everybody else is trying to do means we must pit ourselves and our talents, against other people and their gifts to get our personal slice of the pie. But since nobody can "make it" or "get there" entirely on their own, we've got to rely on other people, including the people we compete against, to help us get to where we want to go. Can anybody say oxymoron?

This seeming contradiction is what compels human beings to form associations, create partnerships, establish trade groups and join unions. This strength in numbers mindset motivates the joiners to combine forces and resources because they think the shared activity will produce a *competitive advantage* for them through their affiliation with a particular group.

It's also what compels people to exclude other folks from the group they've claimed as theirs in the myopic belief that the more people to share resources with, the less there is for them. Exclusion then is seen as another form of *competitive advantage.*

The behavior spawned by the mindset of exclusion for the purpose of acquisition, allocation or control of available resources: *war, ethnic cleansing, genocide, wealth inequality, discrimination, racism, sexism and a host of other societal maladies,* has fostered a system of inequity that has consigned much of the world's population to a "one step forward, two steps back" existence.

This "us against them" mentality, as old as civilization itself, helps to stymie Personal Empowerment because the behavior this mindset produces promotes group membership rather than individual power as the best way to obtain, maintain, sustain and attain. What's more, the "us against them" mindset of competition means that there are no rules in the game.

By any means necessary becomes a way of life. If I have to cheat you to beat you becomes an acceptable value to hold. The end (winning) justifies the means (whatever we have to do) to keep the resources, opportunity and prosperity in the hands of our group and keep them away from yours.

The actions taken by people who share this mindset or embrace this attitude have bastardized the meaning of the word compete. To them compete does not mean to always bring your "A" game. It does not mean to out-perform the other person or other team due to hard work, increased preparation, exceptional skill or superior effort. It doesn't mean to use knowledge, experience, endurance, persistence and perseverance to accomplish the four things most of us are trying to accomplish.

Competition, to people who hold the "all is fair in order to win" viewpoint, literally means doing whatever is necessary to get, keep and grow much more than those they seek to exclude. Win at all costs becomes the driving force. The how becomes irrelevant: *steal from you, cheat you, lie to you, lie on you, block you, discriminate against you, red-line you or dumb you down.* Every and anything is acceptable.

It likely goes without saying that the competitive attitudes I've just described are what keeps most of the world's people at each other's throats and sadly, the United States of America is no exception.

What may be harder to discern though is that once this "anything goes" attitude of competition becomes the predominant point of view in any hierarchical organization, government body, corporation, workplace or school, the individual will then adopt or be infected by that attitude.

Their personality, their actions, positions and beliefs, shaped by the group culture or group leaders may empower the group as a whole, but it will also diminish time spent on personal development and individual growth. The quest for personal power will fall by the wayside as the pursuit for position power within the group is seen as the easiest pathway to achieve *'The Four Things'*.

The lifestyle choice to subjugate personal power for group power is what blinds so many people to the *competitive advantage* provided through maximized potential. To be empowered means to be in control of your own destiny and able to pursue unlimited options. Options conceived through your mindset and unshackled by the whims, wants or worries of someone with whom you must compete or someone you're dependent on.

In most group associations, an individual can only go as far or climb as high as the other members allow. More importantly, the associate body are the givers of power within the group which also means that they can take the power away.

The conscious decision to "go along to get along" as a strategy to attainment may seem a surer or quicker way to success but it doesn't eliminate the need to compete. In actuality, it intensifies competition for positions of dominance or influence within the association, and often sets members at odds with each other or results in cliques and conflict as members fight for power within the group.

Climbing the organizational ladder to a perceived position of power is a poor substitute for the actual personal power supplied by a person's enormous potential because it limits possibilities. Self-generated personal power on the other hand is self-contained *and* self-controlled. Personal power is produced and directed by the individual and ignited by their personal desire to create limit-less opportunities.

People who are empowered walk to the beat of their own drum. They decide for themselves which choices to make and opportunities to take. They're often successful in their pursuit of the four things most of us are trying to do because they're confident that they have the best *competitive advantage*: living their purpose.

To be empowered is to have influence and respect. Most of those with the ability to influence other people, or who possess the power to gain another's respect have generally attained a level of prominence, excellence or leadership in their chosen profession. The position they've reached, the challenges they've overcome, and the achievements they've earned give their voices weight. Their actions are seen as examples to follow.

Just like you and I, the people we look to for inspiration and motivation had to compete for their opportunity. Those we admire or try to emulate had to out-do numerous rivals and jump through countless hoops, on a continuous basis, to obtain the position they now occupy. What's more, they have to work like hell to maintain and sustain their position.

Think of the major influencers of our era. People like Oprah, Serena, Jobs, Buffett, Bezos, LeBron, Gates, Zuckerberg, Obama, Musk and Pelosi, to name just a handful. What was their competitive advantage? Was it their talent or their determination? Was it right place at the right time or maybe persistence and tenacity? Could it have been their brilliance and knowledge, or did they use money, and charisma? Perhaps it was their charm or their looks?

It's a safe bet that the people we hold in high esteem, the folks we are willing to be influenced by used all of these things and probably much more to get to where they are and to stay there.

And though I don't personally know any of the influential people I just named, I'm familiar with their stories and suspect that each one of them used their *purpose*, their reason for being here on this planet, as their preeminent *competitive advantage*.

Earlier in this chapter, I mentioned that *To Be Empowered* is to be "in control of your own destiny." In most definitions, destiny refers to a pre-determined state or condition of a person or thing by either the divine will of God or by human will.

In Christian theology, Predestination is a doctrine that all events in a person's life have been set by God, that is, pre-destined or pre-determined by God. Sometimes the word destiny is used as a synonym for the word fate, which essentially means a foreordained future or an unchangeable lot in life. The common denominator to these beliefs is God, as in God is the ultimate decider; the Higher Power through which all things come to pass.

And even though the debate between the concepts of Predestination and its opposite, Self-Determination as a predictor of our destiny has been on-going for centuries, I don't think it is your lot in life, or where you end up in life that is determined by God. I do believe however, that what our Creator pre-determines for us is our *purpose*.

If you're fortunate enough to find your purpose, smart enough to work your purpose and brave enough to live your purpose, you will determine your own fate. You will decide your lot in life.

I was late in coming to understand the power of purpose. I didn't know its value; heck I didn't even know I had a purpose in this world until my mid-thirties. Looking back, I've often questioned what wonders I might have produced if I'd tapped into the concept in my teens or early twenties. What frustrations, which mis-steps or poor choices I could have avoided if I had known, early in life, about the power of *purpose*.

If you get nothing else from this book (and I sincerely hope that's not the case) get this. *There is something that you're supposed to do here.* Something that God wants you to do in your lifetime that makes your world better, its people stronger, or safer, or wiser, or happier, or healthier. There is a reason that you were chosen to be born. An opportunity to teach or heal; a chance to build or invent, innovate or help, motivate or counsel, nourish and love.

There is a reason why your specific sperm cell hit your specific egg to produce the unique and specific you. There is no one expressly like you on this planet. If you can tap into the essence of you, if you can discern and understand your God-given purpose, you will then become an insurmountable and relentless force.

Take a minute to re-read the definition of destiny on the previous page. Note the part that says, "destiny refers to a pre-determined state or condition of a person or thing by either the divine will of God, *or by human will.*"

I submit that it is human will not God's will that determines the living conditions that have resulted in misery for many of the human beings trying to accomplish *'The Four Things'*.

It was human will that created and perpetuated the African slave trade. Human will that colonized the globe in search of riches to control. Human will that either subjugated or annihilated indigenous people and their societies. Human will that created countries and borders and wars. Human will that designated some world citizens as inferior or unworthy. Human will that polluted the oceans and the air.

It was human beings, not their Creator, that established the competitive doctrine of "by any means necessary"; not for the purpose of controlling *their* destiny, but to wield the power of controlling *yours* by acquiring and allocating the resources and riches found in our world. This human behavior is what determines another human being's "lot in life." To withstand or overcome this human behavior is why people need to be empowered.

The power of *purpose* is in what it produces in a person's life: joy, contentment, meaning and challenge. *Purpose* focuses an individual, reduces distractions, mitigates uncertainty or self-doubt and reinforces one's connection to their Higher Power.

Living your purpose eliminates the toxic emotions of envy of another's possessions or jealousy of what someone else has been able to achieve. Working your purpose reduces the need to "keep up with the Jones," work unsatisfactory jobs, binge-watch video programming, destroy your options with booze or drugs, cheat or cause conflict, or hate on somebody because they got the opportunity you thought you deserved.

Living and working your purpose generates personal power because it removes the need to go along to get along in order to earn your bread or accomplish 'The Four Things'. It means that people won't be able to compromise your values or co-opt your future to do their bidding. It also means that you're beholden to no one except your God, your family and yourself.

People that live and work their purpose compete in an arena of their choosing and employ their individual talent, which is often an indicator of that purpose. They compete against a smaller sub-set of people, people whose interests and talents are similar to theirs. Because they want to win, they bring their "A" game.

For all these reasons, working your purpose provides the *ultimate competitive advantage* because when you compete you've got to win more than you lose in order to have a shot at the title. If you lose more than you win you will quit. If you quit you'll never be able to do any of 'The Four Things', let alone win at the game of life.

I was late to the table in understanding all of this, but eventually I got it. When I did is when I started to soar. When I stopped chasing the money, the possessions and the personal recognition (the media driven image of the so-called "good life"), is when I actually started to have a good life, a purpose driven life.

To be empowered means being able to give to others but before you can give you've got to get. With close to eight billion people all trying to get, you need an advantage. Knowing and working your purpose is that *competitive advantage* because of the commitment, focus and single-mindedness it entails and the personal fulfillment and satisfaction that it brings.

CHAPTER SEVEN

WHAT WILL PROVIDE
THE WILL TO COMPETE?

B ack in the day there was a cynical saying making the rounds that epitomized the frustrating struggles and daily challenges many of us were (and still are) dealing with. The saying captured not just the uncertainty and unfairness of life, but also its futility: *"Life's a bitch, and then you die."*

Every time I heard somebody say this phrase or sing it (a number of songs use it as a lyric) my mind said ouch and I winced a bit as if experiencing a sudden jab to the gut. My mental flinch wasn't because of the hurt and human suffering the saying made evident though. My mind said ouch because of the chronic pain this philosophy was sure to cause those who embraced or believed it.

Much like the current cliché, *"it is what it is,"* "life's a bitch, and then you die" indicates a mindset of passive acceptance of the status quo's unchanging response to either injustice or favoritism: "that's just the way it is". It's also a tacit acknowledgement of an individual's inability to change their current condition, their ultimate fate or their lot in life.

Imagine if Abraham Lincoln, the Wright Brothers, Martin Luther King Jr, Lyndon Johnson or Gloria Steinem had thought this way. Consider where we'd be if Andrew Carnegie, or Henry Ford, Caesar Chavez or Walter Reuther, Malcolm X or Rockefeller believed this. Suppose Bell and Marconi, Tesla and Ghandi, Harriet Tubman and Mother Theresa embraced the mindset of "it is what it is"? What would our world look like now?

Life is *never* "what it is", it is *always* what is still to come. That's why people compare life to a journey. A lifelong excursion that *can* sometimes be a "bitch" but can also be a fabulous trip if you've got an up-to-date map, an accurate GPS, the will to "go for it" and the ability to make something happen!

Life is not a destination. It's not the finishing point, it's not the end of the trip. Life *is* the trip. The futility of life, *"and then you die"*, is simply a self-defeating feeling of *"what's the use"* caused by a sense of powerlessness to control not just our inevitable death, but our finite, precious life.

Death is only the culmination, the final stop on our journey of life. A final destination that despite our differences, our wealth or position we all will reach and are equally unable to control.

Life on the other hand is what we make it. Life is not equal. The fate of our death may be out of our hands, but the destiny of our life is ours to command. "It is what it is" relates only to our pre-destined end, our final destination, not our journey.

Life *is* a bitch if you do not win when you compete, which is why it helps to have the competitive advantage of purpose. Life *will* be a guaranteed bitch if you give up before you start or quit before you finish. Life is a continuous bitch, with constant disappointments if one is afraid or ill-equipped to compete for *'The Four Things'*.

With almost eight billion competitors in the arena of life, with all the diversity of experience, talent and knowledge to contend with; the desire to compete, the *will* to get in there and battle for what you need and want is critical to success. Without this determination, this resolve to engage the competition, there will be little chance of winning consistently, and no chance to control your fate.

To compete against a quality opponent is tough. Winning repeatedly over a long period of time is even tougher. Consequently, some people are reluctant to compete, or afraid to try, or don't want to risk failure so they refuse to enter the arena. Other folk will do unscrupulous, illegal or nefarious things in order to win or reduce the competition.

Some of us, intent on control of resources or maintaining the status quo, actively discourage competitive will in people and squelch their desire to compete. Because competition is so strenuous and intense, many people are eager to trade their need to compete for the seeming security of a go along to get along existence, hopeful that they'll get lucky by association.

That's why, *"life's a bitch, and then you die"* resonates so clearly to so many. That's why, "it is what it is" has become a mindset shield, used to block the disappointment of those unwilling to compete for the right to control their destiny.

To be Empowered means to know more than those who would keep you down or *out of the game.* So, let me clue you in on what the 'Controllers' and 'Maintainers' don't want you to know; what they'd much prefer be kept quiet. Let me amplify what the wise teachers, the righteous preachers, the change-agents and motivators have been telling us for years: DREAM BIG!

Big Dreams are tremendously powerful because Big Dreams provide the *will to compete* and the discipline to stay the course. Big Dreams supply the motivation, determination and inspiration to *want* to compete. Big Dreams offer direction for your life and form the parameters of your journey. Big Dreams develop the roadmap to follow to discover your purpose and control your destiny.

In some ways life is like a jigsaw puzzle. The vast majority of us enters life with all the pieces to correctly complete their individual puzzle of life. But like most puzzles, there are no instructions as to which piece goes where or even which piece of the puzzle connects to another. Experienced puzzle solvers know that an effective strategy is to complete the borders first, connect other key pieces to that border, then fill in the remainder.

The borders to our life's puzzle are the four elements to maximized potential: *Mindset, Behavior, Action Steps and Individual Planning.* These borders shape our lives and supply the connections that result in a correctly completed puzzle.

Our key pieces: *Curiosity, Talent, Big Dreams* and *Purpose* link to the border pieces then the puzzle fills in using the twelve Empowerment Principles discussed in chapter four (more input on this in the chapters ahead).

Unlike most static jigsaw puzzles however, even if our border pieces (the four elements to maximized potential) are accurately placed, the key pieces are properly linked, and the empowerment pieces are connected correctly, the life puzzle of empowered people never gets completely filled in. They remain a "work in progress" because empowered people add new pieces to their life puzzle throughout their life journey.

Empowered people *never quit* trying to "Max-Their-Po". They *never quit* learning, so they *never quit* growing. They *never quit* doing because they *never quit* dreaming. Most empowered people's journey of life ends before their puzzle of life is completed because the power of their Big Dream challenges, pushes and sustains them for a *lifetime* as they strive to realize their greatness through action.

Most of the empowered people I've known, worked with or studied have never even thought that "life's a bitch, and then you die" because their Big Dreams provided them the will to compete and the desire to win.

They've never bought into "it is what it is" because their Big Dreams motivated them to keep it moving forward and work for personal and societal transformation. They've rarely had to "go along to get along" because their Big Dream set the direction for their life.

Big Dreams are an immense catalyst to individual and social growth, which means they are also an enormous threat to the status quo. Big Dreams destabilize the 'Controllers', disrupt the 'Maintainers' and energize individual action. Big Dreams power life itself and ignite the change an evolving world demands.

If you haven't yet discovered your purpose in life your Big Dream can help you find it. If you can't decide which direction to take or career to pursue your Big Dreams can point the way. Your Big Dream will get and keep you focused, guide your behavior and direct your action. It will also provide the objectives for your plan, and the blueprint to follow to build a successful, rewarding life. It will enhance your chance to achieve the four things just about everybody on the planet is trying to do.

But here's the thing about Big Dreams. Sometimes they are as fragile as gossamer wings or fine crystal and can be shattered with minimal pressure. Often, because Big Dreams upset the existing order of things, people try to stop or derail them, or lay a trap for the people who dream them.

That's one of the reasons why the twelve *'Empowerment Principles'* are essential pieces in your puzzle of life. To be empowered means to recognize and avoid the traps that block progress, halt momentum and deprive an individual of both their competitive advantage and their will to compete.

CHAPTER EIGHT

THE DREAM STEALERS

Much as people try to claim otherwise, our world is not really designed to promote or encourage an individual's big dreams. Our societal systems are much more likely to reward individuals that contribute to the sustainability of the organization, the company or the state than it is to reward or celebrate people who chase their dreams.

Until that is, they catch them. Then the naysayers and those that said "it couldn't be done" jump on the dreamer's bandwagon in hopes that some of the glory will rub off on them.

If you are fortunate to live in a Pro-Democracy/Free Enterprise country, the motivating myth of the iconoclastic dreamer with an innovative idea, and the plan, pluck and cash to succeed by making a difference, is a fate we're told is possible for us all, regardless of our position on the totem pole.

But if you're not fortunate and must reside and operate under an autocratic, communist, or authoritarian regime big individual dreams are discouraged, if not out-right criminalized. They're extremely difficult to realize because big dreams rock the boat of the leadership class and those who would keep things as they are.

In countries that have adopted and embraced a quasi-Socialist-Democratic system of governance, where production of resources and the wealth it generates are collectively owned by the people, the needs of each individual are also the collective responsibility of all the people. Opportunities to realize big dreams are limited and rare in these countries because they need workers to keep it all going more than they want dreamers who seek to change it.

It's one thing to have a big dream. It's another thing entirely to make that big dream come true, especially since there are *dream stealers* seemingly lurking on every corner and hanging around every bend of your life journey, regardless of the system of governance or nation in which you reside.

In our youth, most of us spent hours daydreaming about doing exciting, fabulous and momentous things with our lives. We fantasized about acquiring superhuman abilities, exploring mysterious, exotic places, becoming famous and influential or amassing riches and the trappings of power.

Some of us contrive extremely personal dreams like escaping poverty or a brutal and unjust government regime, finding steady employment or attracting someone to love. Still more dream of buying a plot of land, building a home and raising a family. Others have revolutionary dreams like eradicating racism, ending homelessness, reversing the effects of climate change, and colonizing the planet Mars.

In most cases, but certainly not all, as we mature and grow older our big dreams recede into the background of our consciousness as the day to day details of basic survival become top of mind. The majority of people whose big dreams have faded become the *"settlers"* I spoke of in chapter four, unaware that they've lost not just their dreams but also the *competitive will* those dreams provide.

The unfortunate fact behind the faded dreams of most of those who've settled, is that their dreams weren't willingly abandoned. They didn't forsake them or forget them. They were *forced* to settle because their dreams could not be made real. Their dreams couldn't be realized because they became ensnared in the traps installed by the *dream stealers*.

When I envision a trap, I picture a human-made contraption or device constructed to catch an animal. Its purpose is to ensnare a critter in order to kill it, eat it, remove it or profit from it. For a trap to be effective it must be concealed, deliberately hidden. To catch the prey in the snare and to secure it, the animal one wishes to capture must unwittingly ensnare *itself* allowing the trap setters to return later to do with it what they choose.

I've seen bear traps, wolf traps, rabbit traps, mouse traps, racoon traps and fish traps up close and personal. I've seen jungle movies where villagers dug deep pits, inserted sharpened sticks then obscured the hole with ground cover to catch and eliminate the big cats that preyed on them. I've seen war movies where the same type of traps were utilized to snare and kill enemy combatants. I've seen westerns where the cowboys herd and corral wild horses and ponies into a one-way-in, one-way-out box canyon.

The objectives of the trap setters vary, but encompass the general categories of elimination, dominance, personal safety and resource acquisition. Ranchers and growers utilize traps to eliminate predators intent on eating their livestock and produce. People set traps for rodents and vermin to remove them from their midst. We set traps for bears and large mammals that we fear and wish to control. Some lay traps to eat what they catch, while others set traps to sell what they've captured.

Habitually, traps are laid to seize animals from which to profit. Fishermen put down traps to feed the people. Poachers arrange traps for elephants and rhinos to harvest their ivory tusks and horns. Some folks have trapped beaver, mink and foxes, to the point of extinction, to take their fur to sell as hats, coats and gloves.

Most of the time humans place traps to *eliminate the competition.* The rancher hides wolf traps because he competes with the wolf for his cattle. The warrior establishes traps for his enemy to eliminate soldiers from the battlefield. The farmer puts out traps for the rabbits to stop them from consuming his crops before he can sell them.

For a trap to entice what it is meant to capture, there must be a lure, something to attract the prey and pull it in. Bear traps baited with grease and carbs, wolf traps baited with fresh wild meat, fishhooks baited with wriggly, squiggly live creatures.

Highly efficient traps combine a sensory lure, maximum concealment and the means to secure and contain the subject of the trap until it is removed. What happens next depends on motive. It could be eaten, exterminated, or stripped of its meat, hair or skin. But if the thing is really scary, if we think we can't *compete against it,* that it might beat us, most likely it will be killed.

A sizeable percentage of the people who've settled, whose big dreams were never realized, unwittingly fell prey to one or more of the *dream stealers* traps. These *dream stealers* aren't interested in eating their catch or wearing its body parts though. Their traps have been laid for one primary reason; to remove another *human being* from the competitive mix so their odds of winning are increased.

For those who would compete, traps are scattered throughout the landscape like IED's in a war zone. And just like a land-mine, these traps, when triggered will blow to smithereens the dreams of any competitor unwary enough to encounter them.

Traps like addiction to booze, drugs, porn and sex. Seductive traps baited with lures that lead to felony convictions, incarceration and disenfranchisement.

Tight fitting, almost inescapable traps like teenage pregnancy, domestic violence victimhood, unpaid child support and financial obligations in default. Sharp toothed traps that entice with the intoxicating lure of easy and fast attainment, set by con artists intent on deceiving or tricking unsuspecting dupes out of their resources.

Harmless looking traps with no keys, invisible locks and no apparent way out, laid by trusted associates and people who claim to 'know what's best'. "I wouldn't do that if I were you", these *dream stealers* caution upon hearing someone's big dream. "You'll only be setting yourself up for failure. Best to stay in your own lane," they discourage "I just don't want you to be hurt".

I call these examples *dream stealers* and compare them to traps because they remove the competitor from the game. Snares like these, hidden in plain sight, entangle their captives and keep them locked in place.

Getting out of any of these traps leaves its captive so mangled, exhausted and frustrated that their energy and their *will to compete* has already been spent in the effort to break free. *Settling* for, or "that's good enough", becomes the predominant mindset of those who've escaped and consequently, another big dream is never realized.

Of all the traps in all the world, irrespective of the system of government, perhaps the greatest are the two that pose the most difficulty to conceiving or realizing big individual dreams: fear and ignorance. Fear, as in lacking the courage and self-confidence to go make the dream come true. Ignorance, as in not having the knowledge or self-awareness to know what is possible to achieve or how to go get it.

To be Empowered means to have options and choices. To keep your options open and to have multiple choices in life you must avoid the *dream stealers* and steer clear of the traps. It's highly unlikely that you'll be able to obtain, maintain, sustain and attain much of anything if you lack the will or ability to compete.

Chasing a *Big Dream* provides that will while working your *Purpose* supplies the competitive advantage. You need both will and advantage to compete because you've *got* to win more than you lose otherwise the tendency is to "throw in the towel".

What will keep you in the game incorporates three things: what you know, what you do and what you are. These components produce *the winning combination*, provide the agility to side-step any trap and develop the ability to repel each of the *dream stealers* especially the hardest to avoid, the "twin traps" of fear and ignorance.

CHAPTER NINE

TO WIN CONSISTENTLY
AVOID THE TWIN TRAPS

"What is fear," I asked my classroom full of returning citizens (formerly referred to as ex-cons). "False Evidence Appearing Real" replied one fellow, repeating what many incarcerated people hear in group sessions meant to rehabilitate them.

"What is fear," I asked my cohort of 11th and 12th graders. "It's when you're really scared" answered a young lady. "No it's not," a teenaged boy countered, "fear is what makes you a coward."

"What is fear," I asked my roomful of community college students. "It's when you're afraid to take the test," someone ventured. "I wouldn't know" someone else said, "I ain't afraid of nothing"!

"What is fear," I asked my all female group gathered to provide support to domestic violence survivors. "It's a dread I always felt when my man would come home drunk," said one. Another replied, "Fear is the worry I have when I can't feed my kids." "It's like a panic attack," a third lady added, "like when I can't afford my medication."

To all these replies, my response never varied. "Yes" I affirmed, "but what *is* fear? I'm not asking you for a synonym for the word, or what makes you fearful or doesn't. I'm asking for the definition of the word. Tell me what fear is by telling me what the word means."

No one ventured an answer, but I could sense their brains whirring as they tried to figure out where I was going with this line of questioning. By this time in my Empowerment Project Course, we'd moved out of the *Mindset* module and moved into *Behavior*. Usually at this point in the curriculum, we'd developed an easy rapport in the classroom and most of us were comfortable with each other. Still, no one was willing to speak up and risk embarrassment, fearing ridicule from their peers if they got the definition wrong.

To ease the tension, I tossed the dictionary I always carried to one of the students in the second row. "Give us the definition will you please" I asked, then turned to the whiteboard and began to write FEAR in big block letters, using a red marker to underline the word with a flourish. By the time I'd finished, the student I'd put on the spot was ready with the definition.

FEAR IS AN UNPLEASANT EMOTION I wrote as my pupil read the meaning in a voice that carried throughout the room; CAUSED BY THE ANTICIPATION OF PAIN OR THE NEARNESS OF DANGER.

Turning around to face the class I emphasized, "that's it. That's all fear is, an emotion like joy and sadness, anger and jealousy are emotions. The emotion of fear comes upon us when we think that something is likely to happen that will put a hurt on us in some way; psychologically, physically, or financially. Similarly, the emotion of fear arises when we think that something or someone presents a danger or threat to our personal safety, our security, our family and loved ones."

Animatedly starting to pace the room, in full teacher mode I continued the lecture, "notice the words ANTICIPATION and NEARNESS in the definition. Fear rises in us when we *foresee* that we *might* be hurt. The emotion of fear washes over us when we *suspect* danger could be near or *predict* in advance, based on a *feeling*, that the likelihood of vulnerability is high.

Note also that the definition doesn't include certainty. It doesn't say that pain *will* be caused or that danger *is* near, only that it's possible. Let me put it plainly. Fear rises in us based on *maybe's*, built on *might's* and grounded in *could's*. Fear envelops us in most cases created by false data shaped by a closed mindset. Fear's *maybe's* limit action. Fear's *might's* block progress. Fear's *could's* stop big dreams."

My reason for sharing these actual classroom conversations here in these pages is to illustrate the point that a whole lot of people, desperate to accomplish the four things almost everybody on the planet is trying to do, have never even considered the meaning of fear. Consequently, they've rarely understood the enormous impact the emotion of fear has on the ability to maximize individual potential.

People who fear that someone or something might hurt them become reluctant to engage others and withdraw from the competition. Folks who fear that unfamiliar places, unknown faces or humans of different races may present a physical or emotional danger, wall themselves off to protect what they suspect *may* be at risk.

Most who mis-use the fear emotion block their ability to achieve greatness because their mindset is confused by suspicion, their behavior is altered by distrust and their actions are corroded by self-interest. Their individual plan rarely gets implemented due to self-doubt or an absence of confidence.

The lack of awareness of fear's purpose has far reaching implications for anyone that is trying to change, create, develop, improve or initiate a project, a program or venture. Without a clear and thorough understanding of how to utilize the fear emotion, people often fail to see fear for what it actually is; a master trap, artfully hidden, easy to fall into, incredibly tough to escape from and equipped with shackles on the mind that hold its victims tight.

So then, what is the purpose of fear? Why does our mind make our pulse race, our heart beat faster, our senses heighten, our nerves tingle when we experience the emotion of fear? To get us moving that's why, to get us out of physical danger, out of harm's way. To make sure we don't experience the pain we *anticipate* will be caused by that danger, and to allow us to survive the day.

Fear is not meant to stop us from doing. It is not meant to obstruct us or make us give up or defeat us. The fear emotion's purpose is not to cause trepidation when trying out for the team or speaking publicly in a group setting. It's not intended to create apprehension when asking for a date, flying in an aircraft or admitting you can't read well.

Fear is meant to get us moving fast! It's meant to produce immediate action to change our current circumstance, avert a precarious situation, or eliminate exposure to a toxic or life threatening environment. Fear's reason for being is to keep us from being *physically* hurt not mentally wounded. That's why it's essential to maximize individual potential because operating on all cylinders results in a strong mental attitude.

Yet despite the widely held idea most Americans have been taught, that we're not supposed to let fear stop us, many haven't internalized the message because they've misunderstood fear's purpose. They let fear of rejection, fear of ridicule, fear of failure and even fear of success immobilize them. They allowed fear of being gossiped about, fear of being ostracized or fear of being humiliated to stop them from walking to their personal beat and determining their own fate.

Here's the thing. To successfully navigate a world in which other people's emotions impact the group, most of us have learned that we have to control our own. We've learned that to exhibit anger makes others defensive, fearful or uncertain, so we control our anger. We've come to know, that to get along with other people, disgust is a counterproductive emotion, so we keep it to ourselves. We've discovered that in certain situations it's best not to act surprised or exhibit sadness, so we control those emotions by masking them.

Fear is no different than the other emotions in this regard. To master our fear, to make sure it does not stop us we've got to *control* our fear by activating our courage. We then use that courage as a shield to hold back the fear!

Courage is not the absence of fear. Courage doesn't eliminate fear. Courage doesn't make a person fear-less. Courage serves as a barricade to fear, it counters the fear and blocks it. Courage allows one to stay focused, strong and positive. It helps us to keep it moving regardless of the fear, worry or apprehension a situation provokes.

To activate our courage we've got to reach inside ourselves and pull out our purpose, our perception, our confidence, our wisdom, our empathy, our persistence. Then we use the courage these attributes will unleash to control the urge to flee or to hide that fear often produces. We use the courage these traits deliver to encourage and strengthen our will to fight and our ability to persevere.

Because I teach personal empowerment, I've learned that to be empowered means a lot of things, but most of all it means to know. To know the truth, to know yourself, to know your purpose on this earth and to know how to use your talent to win when you compete.

While it is true that knowledge is power, it's also true that power unused is power squandered. To effectively use power consistent action is required. This consistent action and the knowledge, experience and capability it generates, creates immense personal power and helps to boost our confidence high. Unless, that is, an individual falls victim to the trap of fear's twin: ignorance.

I describe fear and ignorance as *"Twin Traps,"* not because they're identical *dream stealers*, but because they are the two greatest obstacles to successful competition. They're twins because the two are connected; ignorance produces fear while fear leads to ignorance.

Ignorance and fear are two sides of the same card that when dealt, effectively tells a player, "don't pass go, don't collect $200, you're out of the game." There is simply no way to win at the game of life if you're fear-filled. There is absolutely no chance of competing successfully if you don't know how the game is played or what steps it takes to win when you compete.

What makes fear and ignorance more confining than most of the other traps scattered throughout our nation and across the world is that once they've ensnared their victim, he, she or they become resigned to remain in the trap to which they've succumbed. They choose an existence of limited opportunities, a life of dissatisfaction and possible despair because it becomes easier to remain hidden in the trap than to claw their way out.

Ignorance, not knowing the who what, where, when, why or how of something mirrors fear's trap because just like fear, the lack of knowledge limits action, blocks progress and stops big dreams.

Though ignorance is often used as a synonym for the word stupidity the words couldn't be more dissimilar. To be ignorant simply means not to know. To be stupid means to know but to choose to go against what you know. A person both ignorant and stupid is all but destined to lose at the game of life even if they were lucky enough to get in on it.

All of us, empowered or not, are ignorant of many things because no one is capable of knowing everything about anything. An ivory tower educator may feel superior to the auto mechanic who struggles with reading, yet the educator is ignorant of what the mechanic knows to fix his car when it breaks down.

Some are ignorant of their history. Some are ignorant of mathematics or science. Others are ignorant of how money works, how to discern truth in Media or what the Constitution of their country actually says. Most of us are ignorant of other people's cultures and customs, religions, languages and spiritual beliefs. This ignorance produces fear of others. The fear of others often derives from not knowing others. Round and round we go straight into the trap.

The default position of many people is to know only what they are interested in and to mainly be interested in only the things that they know. That position is what makes the twin *dream stealers* so successful. The lures that fear and ignorance use to entrap the unwary and keep them out of the competitive mix is why the need for Personal Empowerment is paramount.

To be empowered means being able to start your own ignition. To be empowered also means not being fearful or becoming a victim of the *dream stealers* snare. The power is already inside you to win when you compete, it need only be generated. The fuel to start the process begins with your mindset, but the power is ignited by your behavior. The fuse to your power burns by the actions you take and your ability to recognize and elude the twin traps.

CHAPTER TEN

THE WINNING COMBINATION

What you do (or don't do) will determine the level of success you will experience on your life journey. Who you choose to do it with will also factor into the success equation by influencing your self-esteem, your confidence and the attainment of your goals.

Attainment, as you'll recall from chapter three, is the ultimate objective of the quartet of things most of us on this planet are trying to accomplish: *obtain* the things we need and want, *maintain* the things we've obtained then *sustain* what we've maintained. By accomplishing all three of these universal goals, an individual will have done what he or she set out to do, which is the essence of success. They will have *attained*.

To make these four things happen, and to keep succeeding throughout the entirety of your journey means you'll have to compete for your opportunities, then compete harder to keep them coming, and harder still to increase them.

Most of the globe's eight billion souls whom we compete against, people who strive for continuous or limitless opportunity by accomplishing the four things, will never be able to attain them all. They won't succeed because either their societal system blocks them from the chance to compete or they block their own opportunity by embracing a negative mindset and falling prey to one or more of the traps which effectively removes them from the game.

Up to this point, I've devoted considerable time to discussing the need for competition. I've suggested that embracing the twelve *Empowerment Principles* offers a competitive edge, that working your *Purpose* provides a competitive advantage, and that *Big Dreams* supply the *will* to compete. I've advised of the *dream stealers* traps set to remove you from the competitive game and warned of the *twin traps* of ignorance and fear, which immobilize action and discourage desire to step into the competitive arena.

Because life is a journey not a destination, unless you are fortunate to inherit a financial windfall or earn millions of dollars at a young age (think superstar entertainers, pro athletes and innovation entrepreneurs), or are able to bank sufficient resources to sustain your existence to its end, you will need to compete for decades. As previously noted, if you don't win consistently, if you're not victorious early and often you'll most likely give up or give in.

For those intent on maximizing individual potential in their determination to reach *Self-Actualization,* quitting is not a viable option. Staying in the game until the win becomes the primary goal. Improving your odds of winning, so that you come out on top is both the main objective and the expected outcome of the competitive effort.

Let me put it bluntly. The career position, the job, the spot on the team, the prestigious assignment, or the school you desire for yourself or a loved one is wanted by someone else. The house you want to buy, the apartment you'd like to rent, the association you aspire to join and even the Friday night date you hope to make your lifelong mate, is being pursued by someone else. Everything on earth is coveted by someone or everyone so if you want to make it yours you must compete not just to get it, but to keep it.

As mentioned in chapter eight, there are three major forces that interplay with each other to increase the probabilities of winning consistently over a long period of time: *What You Know, What You Do* and *What You Are*. Many would be competitors choose to enter the fray with one or perhaps two of these forces, but rarely do they employ all three.

Those who win consistently and repeatedly have learned the value and recognize the impact of blending knowledge, capability and character to produce a *winning combination*. They understand how to use the concentrated power of this trio to overwhelm the opponent, and simultaneously build confidence and increase competence to win future engagements.

Each of these forces is equally vital to produce the individual qualities needed to win consistently. None of the three is more important than the other since they work in tandem. Yet like most things in life, the process must begin with knowledge, not just to acquire information or accumulate facts, but to increase areas of expertise, reinforce your desire to compete and perhaps most importantly, learn who you are and what you're about. In short, to know yourself, discover your talent and find your purpose in life.

As I've said repeatedly in these pages, to be empowered means to know more than those who would keep you out of the game know. In fact, *Super-Literacy* is the first of my twelve Empowerment Principles because in the 21st century, it's almost impossible to survive, let alone thrive, without it.

To be *Super-Literate* is to be comfortable and supremely competent with the language of course, but also to be knowledgeable of finance and experienced with technology.

To be literate means to be able to absorb written information quickly and easily (like sucking in a drink through a straw), effortlessly comprehend what you've read, accurately retain the content, and discern how best to use what you've learned.

It also means having the knowledge to recognize fact vs. fiction, truth vs. lies and real vs. fake, while simultaneously developing research, writing and other communication skills.

Super-Literacy is why curiosity is so important to the empowerment process. A curious person *wants* to dig deep for all the information. A curious person *needs* to read and learn, watch and learn, listen and learn then share what they've learned. Curiosity and literacy go together like mind and body to support individual development.

Financial literacy means to understand how money works. To grasp the interwoven concepts of taxes, debt, banks, credit, cryptocurrency, barter and investments like stocks, bonds, real estate, precious metals and scarce resources.

Financial literacy includes avoiding pay-day lenders, check cashing services and refusing jobs that pay earnings off the books or "under the table." It also means resisting debt, living below your means, saving at least 10% of your monthly income and providing a portion of that income to charitable purposes.

Technological literacy refers to all things digital as relates to computers and on-line devices. To be technologically literate is to be at ease navigating a world that functions through an internet portal with a Wi-Fi connection. It means to be familiar with Apps and Programs, diverse Operating Systems, software options and cyber security.

In addition, it means to be able to use technology like we once used books, magazines, newspapers, telephones, the Yellow Pages, TV, Radio, Sears, Block Buster, Travel Agents, Banks, the Neighborhood Newsletter and the Grocery Store. It means to be capable of utilizing technology like we formerly used schools, textbooks, and research material to become literate with both the language and the economics.

Super-Literacy boosts proficiency, breeds curiosity and provides the bedrock to a lifetime of personal growth. It augments an individual's ability to not be victimized, hoodwinked or excluded from the game. It obliterates the twin traps of ignorance and fear and replaces them with a sturdy foundation of optimism, self-confidence and unlimited possibilities upon which to build.

As important as *Super-Literacy* is to the creation of a formidable competitor it alone won't make an individual unbeatable. The knowledge afforded by being literate in language, finance and technology only provides understanding and awareness of things, places, events, concepts, theories, facts, established practices, and primarily the existing order of our world. To increase the competitive power *Super-Literacy* supplies another type of knowledge must be added to the mix, the knowledge of self.

Self-knowledge fortifies and strengthens competitive will and determination to win. Self-knowledge provides insight and focus on capabilities and attributes. Self-knowledge stimulates confidence, enthusiasm and clarifies purpose.

To win more than you lose you've got to *know* what you can do, how good you are and where you need to improve. To win more than you lose you've got to *know* your tolerance for pain, rejection or defeat. To win more than you lose you've got to *know* your level of endurance, how far or fast to push yourself and what will make you quit. To win more than you lose you've got to *know* how bad it feels to lose, and you've got to *know* your resiliency, your ability to bounce back. In short, you need to *know* the power inside you!

To be able to know all of this is where the second force to increase the probabilities of winning consistently over a long period of time comes into play: *What You Do.*

CHAPTER ELEVEN

THE TREASURE MAP

When I was a boy growing up on the segregated south side of Chicago, I didn't know anything about Mindset, Behavior, Action Steps and Individual Planning as the essential components to Max-Yo-Po. In fact, I didn't even know what maximizing your potential meant, having never discussed the concept with anyone trying to survive the mean streets of the Windy City.

What I knew about was keeping your eyes moving and senses heightened to recognize danger and avoid people who posed a threat. I knew about running; running from the gangs that sucked in lost boys, running from the junkies who moved like zombies, running from the pushers whose dope was ever present and running from the cops who sought to contain me.

What the authority figures and wise elders advised me to do to protect myself from peril was to remember to "stay in my place" or "be a credit to my race." They told me to not "make waves," to be respectful to "the Whites," not to cuss or swear in public, to never sass or talk back to the grownups, never hit a girl, and above all try to "stay out of trouble."

These folks, who said they were looking out for me and were only concerned with what was good for me, scolded constantly about my behavior, which they warned would someday get me into something I couldn't get out of. To keep me on the straight and narrow, to *scare me straight* they'd tell horrific tales of what happened in the cells of the Cook County jail or the dreadful penitentiary at Joliet, on the outskirts of Chicago.

Reaching my teens in the midst of the civil rights era, I knew nothing about discovering your God-given purpose or finding your God-given talent. I didn't know much of anything relating to fair competition except trying to earn a place on the team. All I knew then was hustling and scuffling for a chance to escape what was then referred to as the slums (or in polite society circles as the ghetto).

My focus as a young man was not on Personal Empowerment or Self-Actualization. Instead, I spent my time searching for a way out of the hell of living in an underworld of despair, fear and resentment. Searching for a way out of the trap set by others; a trap I call *"The Under"*, as in *under-educated, under-employed, under-paid, under-housed, under-the-influence, under privileged, undervalued, under suspicion* and often *under attack* from those who lived inside and outside of the trap I was forced to call home.

To be clear, I wasn't a bad boy. I didn't hurt people or steal from them or try to sell them dope. I was just a poor boy; a scared and worried boy which made me angry. An enraged young man contained in *"the under"* who rebelled against the authority of the system. I talked back to the teachers. I sassed the elders. I cussed out some playmates. I refused to stay in my place. I always made waves and was rarely respectful to anyone, white, black or other. I would not be restrained.

I ran from trouble in the streets but when it caught me I fought back, which got me in trouble with the adults. I played sports, cards and games like I lived life, angry. I hated to lose which made me even angrier, so I fought not to lose then fought some more if I did. I was, as the old-timers warned, headed for a lifetime of hurt.

Books and curiosity saved me. The solace and excitement I found in the libraries and museums of Chicago soothed and inspired me. I may not have been able (yet) to physically escape *"the under"* but I could go everywhere and do anything when engrossed in a book. I could be anything I could dream of being when captivated and exhilarated by exhibits in a museum.

I wrote this book because I had to let you know that whatever is coming in this post COVID-19 world, you'll be able to survive it and thrive. Whatever you want to make happen as our culture evolves in the wake of the pandemic disaster is more probable than possible *if* you focus on your behavior, on what you do.

One of the motivating things about coming to maturity in this American society and its capitalist system, is that I came to know everything I'm laying out for you in these pages over the course of my journey here. Trial and error, mistake, success, failure, success, fallback, move forward, win, lose, compete harder and win some more.

Looking back and examining what happened, what didn't happen, what should have happened, what would have happened and what might have happened in my life, led me to the realization that I'd been able to come up from *"the under"* and achieve *'The Four Things'* because of what I'd acquired through the books, museums, classrooms, gyms, ball fields and corporate arenas: the keys to the castle, the map to the buried treasure and the directions to the place called success.

When I found the treasure map, I used it to discover what would get me out and keep me out of *"the under."* I used it to start climbing and keep striving regardless of what they threw at me to get me out of the game. The map encouraged me to keep going despite the challenges and promised all the riches in the world if I kept moving forward and did not quit. It led me to the castle on the hill and showed me where to find the key that fit all the locks.

Since you're reading my book, I'm going to let you in on the secret and share the details of my treasure map with you. If you follow the steps precisely, not only will you be capable of achieving the four things just about everybody on the planet is trying to do, you'll also be able to Max-Yo-Po, become self-actualized and control your own destiny. I call the map, *Success Equals 'P'*, but before I reveal the map's directions let me briefly tell you how I found it.

During my television career in Detroit Michigan, I became an "in demand" speaker for organizations and groups whose mission was to inspire and motivate youth. As the founder of a media company, and the writer-producer-host of an Emmy Awarded, highly rated TV show I was perceived to be a role model, someone young people could emulate and aspire to become.

I spoke at Career Day seminars and Entrepreneur summits. I appeared at stop the violence rallies and literacy fairs. I lectured in middle schools, high schools, to church groups and community associations and invariably, when the concept of success was the topic, my young audience would always ask the same type questions.

"Are you a millionaire"? "How much money do you make a week"? "Do you drive a Bentley or a Mercedes"? "Do you live in a mansion"? "Do you have your own jet"? "Do you know Oprah Winfrey; do you know LeBron James"?

It quickly became apparent by the repetitive nature and one-track theme of the questioners, that most had no clear concept of success. They equated it with big money, expensive cars, huge homes, rings, bling and having a whole lot of things. I realized that if they had a false notion of what it *meant* to be a success, then they could not possibly know what it *would take* to become successful.

That "light bulb' moment is what led me to consider all the components that went into creating a successful person. I was flabbergasted when I recognized the connection; a majority of the components began with the letter 'P' as in *potential*!

My surprise quickly turned into elation as I understood that what I'd discovered in my contemplation of success was a guide to follow, and that the *'P's to Succeed* could be used like rungs on a ladder to climb from the underworld of failure and hopelessness to the height of success.

Should you choose to lock these sixteen 'P's into your mindset and use them to influence your behavior, to drive *what you do,* your probability of winning consistently throughout your life journey will be exponentially increased. In fact, you'll be almost unbeatable!

SUCCESS EQUALS 'P'

PURPOSE (Dual Meaning)

- Know why you're doing what you're doing and what you expect to achieve by your action. Does your activity increase your options, lead to empowerment or big dream fulfillment? Are you doing it to expand your mind, improve your circumstance, discover your talent or display your brilliance?

- There is something that you're supposed to do here. Something that God wants you to do in your lifetime that makes your world better, its people stronger, or safer, or wiser, or happier, or healthier. There is a reason that you were chosen to be born. An opportunity to teach or heal; a chance to build or invent, innovate or help, motivate or counsel, nourish and love. Discover your *God-given purpose* and use it to determine what you do and to drive your action. When you're working and living your *purpose*, jealousies, petty rivalries, resentments, procrastination, apathy or self-destructive behavior won't block your potential.

PLAN

- To succeed takes a plan. A *written* direction must be established, and steps followed in correct sequence to get to where you're trying to go. Melding personal interests, family obligations, career goals and financial considerations is a difficult proposition. Without a written plan to follow, a life blueprint so to speak, failure in one or more areas of your journey will be the result.

PRIORITIZE

- Do things in order of importance and do the 'heavy lifting' first. Never put off till tomorrow the things you need to accomplish today. Fun, relaxation, games and media are necessary to mental and physical health but should be pursued only after the major objectives of your daily plan have been completed.

PREPARE

- Get ready for *everything* you do. Don't try to "Wing" it or B.S. your way through it. Never show up for anything that you're not ready to win or ace. Put in the mental and physical work before you arrive. *Always* bring your "A" game and be ready for the unexpected.

PARTICIPATE

- Get involved in everything and anything that is sparked by your curiosity. Join organizations, try out for teams, sing in the choir, volunteer with community groups, diversity councils and schools. Take part in neighborhood associations, the PTA, mentor organizations or advocacy efforts for a cause you believe in. Participation helps in identifying purpose and talent. It pinpoints shortcomings, reinforces capabilities, expands knowledge, increases experience, boosts confidence and heightens self-esteem.

PRACTICE

- To win consistently means to be at the top of your game and superior in skill to the competition. To win over a long period of time means that those skills must remain sharpened, honed to a razor's edge. Practice, constant repetitive actions, conducted diligently against like-minded individuals is the only way to enhance your chances, move to the top of the field and win more than you lose.

PRIDE

- Carry yourself with dignity and self-respect. Appear well groomed, appropriately dressed and in control of your emotions at all times. Avoid treating other people with rudeness or condescension. Take joy in your achievements and find comfort in your strengths but beware on your self-satisfaction morphing into arrogance.

PERFORM

- When it's "go" time you've got to show up and be ready to blow the competition or the audience away! At school, at work, in associate groups and even at home with your family, when the bell rings and it's time to step up you've got to 'go for it'! You can't back down especially when all eyes are on you (which is where prepare and practice come into play).

PRAYER

- This relates to finding your God-given purpose. An indicator of that purpose is often another God-given gift, your talent. Prayer is the essential communication between yourself and your Creator. Prayer, to make sure you're on track; prayer to offer thanks for opportunities; prayer to ask for guidance, input and support when times get tough. Prayer acts as a salve to sooth the hurts you encounter in the arena and strengthens your determination to stay in the game.

PERSISTENCE

- Don't quit, stay the course. Don't quit trying despite the obstacles. Don't quit knocking on doors of possible opportunity. Don't give up on your Big Dream. Don't stop going for the win. Don't stop striving for the top. Don't allow doors slammed in your face to discourage you. Believe in your talent and embrace your purpose. Use them like fuel to provide the energy to keep it going until the end. (This is also where prayer comes into play).

PERSEVERANCE

- Sometimes confused with persistence, perseverance means to hold on and endure while you keep striving. It's not easy to keep moving forward in the face of rejection while pursuing a difficult goal. It takes faith, hope, strength and will-power to hold on till the cavalry comes, the objective is met, and the win is secured. It also means to have confidence that a breakthrough will occur as long as you have the fortitude and tenacity to persist.

PERCEPTION

- Vision is the ability to see the world, its people and things with your eyes, and to navigate your environment by being able to see with your eyes what is around you. Perception, from the verb perceive, is the capability to see what is happening around you not with your eyes but through your experience and knowledge. To have an accurate perception is one of the reasons participation is so important because a multitude of life experiences is crucial to its development. It's why travel and education, diverse people and different customs are broadening. These opportunities allow the capacity to *see* without eyes; to *perceive* what is real or fake.

PRINCIPLED

- Relates to individual values and the determination to stand your ground and maintain personal integrity despite pressure from others for you to "go along to get along." An un-principled person will change like a chameleon to do whatever feels right or benefits them at any given time. The old cliché, "a person who stands for nothing will fall for anything," rings true here. (More on this in chapter 12).

PUNCTUALITY

- Be on time all the time. It is far better to be ten minutes early than to be one minute late. A punctual person explains who they are and what they're about without ever having to open their mouth. Punctuality displays respect for others and show-cases time management skills. It indicates reliability, depend-ability and responsibility. A person that respects other people and is responsible, dependable and reliable is, in most cases, someone to be trusted.

POSITIVE PERSONALITY

- Most people are uncomfortable being around whiners, grip-ers and individuals that transmit a negative vibe. Most of us try to avoid people who shoot down other's ideas, opinions, suggestions or experience. Most become annoyed or put off by braggarts, blow-hards, naysayers and know-it-alls. A wel-coming attitude however draws people in. An open, helpful or inquisitive approach combined with genuine interest in another's position or point of view adds to our knowledge base. A can-do, helpful approach to people, up-lifting words and a grateful heart lights a path to opportunity and helps relieve internal stress as we persist and persevere.

PATIENCE

- We've been conditioned to want it all and programmed to want it all now. What's more, we're constantly told that we can get what we want easy, fast and free! But that's hogwash. Life changes don't come fast, they certainly don't come easy and virtually nothing is free. Everything worthwhile takes time, costs money or expends effort. To obtain, maintain, sustain and attain will mean hard, intense work and sometimes will cost your blood, your sweat and leave you in tears. Patience is the act of adjusting your mindset to understand that if you put in the work demanded by the 'P's' everything you desire can come to pass. Fast may be good depending on the occasion but to maximize your potential, slow and steady is better. It takes time to know, understand and fully utilize the power of you.

So there you have it, my map to all the treasure you can find. Call it Success Equals 'P', the P's to Potential or whatever you choose but remember this, to get *all* that you deserve you'll have to put in *all* the work, *all* the time. You will have to infuse *all* sixteen of these power-packed P's into your mindset and use them to drive *all* that you do. Utilize the P's *always* to win consistently when you compete.

CHAPTER TWELVE

WHO R U & WHAT R U ABOUT?

Let me emphasize a few of the points we've addressed to this point to connect some of the dots. In chapter six I described the apparent contradiction (oxymoron) we face in living and working with other human beings. On the one hand, we need to compete against people for our opportunity to achieve *'The Four Things'*. On the other hand, since no one can succeed entirely on their own, we need other people to help us.

In chapter ten I advised that what you do (or don't do) will determine your level of success and cautioned that who you choose to do it with will factor greatly into the success equation by influencing your self- esteem, confidence and goal attainment.

In chapter four I revealed that self-confidence is the bridge that connects Personal Empowerment to Self-Actualization, and explained that self-confidence, a potent blend of awareness, capability and experience is a major component to being able to turn on your power any time you choose. Confidence in your ability *and* your character. Confidence that increases, not only by what you can do, but by *who you are and what you are about.*

That being the case, in a "me first, get mine" world, who do we ask to help us achieve? Who should we allow into our circle to influence our decisions and provide support? How do we decide which individuals to trust with our Big Dream and our self-esteem? How can we determine *before* letting someone in that he or she won't try to steal our dream, betray us in some way, rip us off, cause damage, or derail our chances to do each of '*The Four Things*'?

Are there tell-tale signs that someone is risky or that somebody is true? How does one decide the value of another individual to their life?

Actually, there's only one answer to all the questions posed in the paragraph above. *Before you can know me, you've got to know you.* Before you can be sure who I am and what I'm about, you've got to know for certain, who you are and what you're about. In other words, you've got to know your values.

Let's be real. People are lying to us constantly it seems like, people from all walks of life. Government officials lying to promote an agenda. Politicians lying to obtain or maintain power. Preachers lying to get or grow their congregation. Con Artists lying to get what we're trying to keep. Spouses and significant others lying in order to stray. Educators lying to push a particular point of view. Law enforcers lying after abusing their power. Media companies and News organizations lying to attract an audience. Crooks lying to evade prison. Children lying to parents to avoid being punished. Parents lying to their children to pacify or keep them in line. Businesspeople lying to increase profits.

Some humans are so intent on using the lie as either a survival mechanism or a competitive tool that they will lie when the truth would work better. Some lie by commission, deliberately making false statements that they know to be untrue ('I did not have sex with that woman'). Others lie by omission, deliberately leaving out facts so as not to incur a negative consequence caused by their action. "I need to take a couple days off," the worker tells the boss by phone. "I had a car accident." What he doesn't add is that he drove drunk and hurt himself. He left that part out, hoping to prevent an adverse response, like getting fired.

Why so many lies? It's about behavior. A lot of people lie to try to cover up what they did or are currently doing. They lie because they don't want their actions known ("I've never used illegal drugs") or because they don't want to pay the price ("I didn't do it, I'm innocent"). Many lie to make themselves seem accomplished ("I've got three degrees" says the high school dropout) or to take advantage of someone ("this is a once in a lifetime investment"). Some lie because they're ashamed of their actions (I didn't beat my wife), while still more lie to shift blame ("two Black guys did it"). People lie to cheat; they lie to entrap, and they lie to boast because they think it will help them win ("I got the most votes, but the election was stolen").

It is no lie that scoundrels abound in our midst, in fact it's indisputably true. A realistic yet cynical viewpoint could justifiably be formed that with all the rip-offs surrounding us no one can be trusted, which sets up the oxymoron I mentioned at the top of this chapter: *since no one can succeed entirely on their own, we need other people to help us.* How do we choose, how do we know who or what is right for us? We look to our values and find those who share them.

It is a fact that your mindset, the way you think drives your behavior, what you do. But it's also fact that what you do derives in large measure from who you are and what you're about, *your values.* Some people lie and cheat but not all people. Some steal and hurt but a lot more don't. With almost eight billion of us all trying to make their journey it's inevitable that some will choose the wrong way. It's just as inevitable that a lot of them embrace what you are about. It's a safe bet that a whole lot of people hold the same value system as yours.

Far too often when I've been in classrooms teaching my Empowerment Project curriculum I have been stunned by the number of students who have never considered the impact values have on their life trajectory. Truth be told, a majority of them confused the word value for the word values, and in so doing were unaware of each word's meaning and purpose.

"Who wants to tell us the difference between the words value and values," I ask to begin the dialogue for the day's session. After working with them for a couple of weeks by this time in the Program, I can usually anticipate a spirited exchange when I throw out a talking point. But on this question, the response I typically get from them is a look that says, 'don't ask me'.

"Come on," I coax "somebody tell me, tell us what the word value means." A brief flurry of responses ultimately yields the correct answer. 'Worth' someone replies, 'the value of something is what it is worth'. "Right on," I bark enthusiastically. "Now who sets the value, the buyer or the seller"?

"The buyer," a lady quickly asserts. "The seller," retorts a guy sitting behind her. "The seller," a young woman says, agreeing with the guy. "Nuh-uh" responds an older gentleman shaking his head from side to side, "the seller sets the price, the buyer determines the value."

"Bingo," I say, nodding assent to the man. "You nailed it! The seller establishes how much something costs, but the buyer decides if it is worth it! Remember that the next time you interview for a job or go for a promotion," I caution with a smile.

"OK then" I continue, still looking at the man but really talking to every student in the room. "What about values, what does that word mean"? No answers greet my question. "Let me put it to you this way" I prod, moving close enough to touch each student in the cohort and look into their eyes, "*who are you and what are you about?*"

I watch silently awaiting a response and notice them glance at each other to see who would answer; everyone worried that I would call on them. Finally, someone breaks the silence with a question, "what do you mean, Mr. Miller," prompting a statement from another, "never thought about it", then one more, "what does who I am and what I'm about have to do with the worth of something?"

Teaching is a two way street. The instructor gives valuable information to the student to use in their development. In return, the student offers the teacher input on that info and feedback on their grasp of the subject matter. If both are doing their jobs properly, each adds to the other's knowledge and understanding.

The reason I was (and continue to be) stunned by my students lack of comprehension, as to what I'm probing for with the word values, is that it illustrates with clarity why there are so many successful liars, deceivers, cheaters, crooks and fools in our competitive arenas.

Put simply, a whole lot of individuals don't have a clue as to what they're about. Consequently, they don't recognize the unscrupulous competitor whose behavior is predicated on doing anything they think will help them win. They can't identify devious people who would use any trick in the book to get the opposition out of the game. Individuals that will do any deed necessary to rig the competition or manipulate the odds in their favor.

To fall for what value-less people like this are attempting is to become a victim of their deception. To circumvent their traps means being able to quickly size them up and demands an understanding of their motives, who they are, and what they're about. That input is then weighed, examined and evaluated for its perceived value (worth) based on the mindset of the would be victim (is there something in it for me?).

What my students teach me, what they help me to understand is why the Con men and women, with the Ponzi schemes, the Internet scams and the Identity thefts are so prevalent. People can and will go along with just about anything if they don't know what they stand for. They will and do give themselves up to other's ambitions if they don't know who they are. And the only way to know those things for certain is to know your values, like you know your name.

Values are the principles you've chosen to embrace that influence your thoughts (mindset) and drive what you do (behavior). *Mindset* and *Behavior* are two of the four elements to maximized potential, so the correlation is clear between the importance of values to a *Self-Actualized* life.

Your core values shape your character and constitute what's important to you internally, what you believe in and what you stand for. They form what you aspire to become. Values determine your code of honor, your code of conduct and set the lines you will not cross.

As my friend, the late sociologist, Dr. Lynn Lewis explained during a TV show I produced titled 'Who Let the Greed In, Who Let the Values Out' (2003)

> *"There once was a time when there was a high premium placed on non-material cultural values such as integrity, ethics, morals, beliefs, dignity...and what you have happening*

now is a tremendous emphasis on material cultural values
such as I'm going to define myself by what's on my back, and
what's on my feet, and what's around my wrist, and what's
on my fingers; as opposed to what's in my head, and what's
in my heart, and what's in my character."

A person's character is created, nourished and fortified by their individual values. Character evolves as values change. Values change with increased knowledge, experience and exposure to different people, places and things. An individual not grounded in personal values navigates the journey of life without a compass or guide and can choose the wrong way or be led astray by anyone they decide to follow (can anybody say Q-Anon).

Values are not the same as morals. Morals relate to behavior that is either right or wrong based on religious beliefs, ethnic customs or conventional wisdom. The entire concept of morality has been clouded for centuries due to the diametrically opposed interpretation of what it means to be moral.

For some individuals, to do the moral thing is to do the *"right"* thing; the Ten Commandments type things, or the Golden Rule thing: "Do unto others as you would have them do unto you." However, for most world governments and the people who administer them, *Might Makes Right*. Whoever has the most money, the superior weaponry, the most land or most people, whoever is the *mightiest* group, determines for everyone else what is the right thing to do. This mindset has supplanted the Golden Rule with an alternative message: "He who has the gold rules."

Values though are not governed or decided by the mightiest among us. Values are independently acquired. Each individual decides which principles to choose and embrace to guide their actions. Our values may be formed through the input of others (parents, teachers, co-workers, friends, spouses), or influenced by those of people we admire, but value acquisition is a uniquely personal choice.

In my *Empowerment Project* curriculum, I focus on twenty-one "winning values" that help to strengthen the power inside. Once obtained these values (or Principles as discussed in chapter 11, Success equals 'P') will maintain for a lifetime. They'll sustain you through the good times and the challenging, worrying times.

By incorporating them into your mindset and your daily grind you will learn who to let into your circle and whom to exclude. You will discover who is worthy of your trust and who is not. You'll know who to rely on for help. You'll know who won't try to rip you off and you will always know, just like you know your name, who you are, and what you're about.

THE WINNING VALUES

Integrity – Honesty – Loyalty – Sharing – Thrift –
Mentoring – Education – Family First – Punctuality –
Forgiveness – Cleanliness – Responsibility – Super-Literacy –
Industriousness – Word As Bond – Healthy Habits –
Higher Power – The Golden Rule – Entrepreneurship –
Honor Commitments – Fair Play

I'm not suggesting that you adopt my winning values as your own, but I am advising that you determine your own. Use your values to further develop your character but use them primarily to gauge compatibility with people you think will help you win.

Guilt or failure by association is an unfortunate but real phenomenon. Success by association, though not a given, is probable if you associate with, partner with or join with people that share your core values. To minimize risk to your health, wealth, peace of mind, confidence and self-esteem choose and display your values and avoid people that do not share them.

Which is why I say before you can know who I am, you've got to know *who you are*. Before you can know what I'm about, you've got to know *what you're about*.

CHAPTER THIRTEEN

YOU CAN'T GET THERE BY YOURSELF

It is a well-known fact that there is power in numbers. What's not so well known is that the power in other people can be fueled and controlled by the power inside you.

I've written at length about *'The Four Things'*, mostly in the context of why they're so hard to accomplish, our human desire to do all four, and the necessity to continuously compete to get the things we need and want, keep the things we get, grow what we've been able to keep and succeed through every step of life's journey.

A large portion of our human need and much of our human desire is more dependent on connecting with other individuals than it is on the acquisition of things, possessions, money or status, however. Truth be told many people seek to acquire fame, recognition and the trappings of wealth as a lure to attract other people; to use the notoriety of their lofty position to bring others into their orbit.

Our desires to form a bond with other people, to fall in love, cherish and nourish a family, and to feel the warmth that acceptance and belonging radiates is a much stronger motivator than is our need for life's material things. The vast majority of us want *and* need to get, keep and grow relationships with people. We want to network, form associations and be a part of something that makes us feel special, important and necessary.

What's more, this need for companionship, friendship and human connection is not a short-term or transitory need. It is essential for the entirety of our journey here, every bit as important to our wellbeing as air, food, and water.

In fact, as the psychologists have discovered, much of the dissatisfaction, depression, apathy or angst experienced by so many of our fellow travelers is due primarily to the loneliness or incompleteness felt by those whose relationship needs are unmet or unfulfilled.

This emptiness, this feeling of *something lacking* creates anxiety, uncertainty and generates additional feelings of self-doubt and frustration. The void produced by discontent that people feel must be filled with something and far too many choose to fill it with behavior like addiction, violence, or crime that will ultimately entrap them and keep them out of the game.

The universal human need to unite with other humans confronts an unmistakable reality, *people don't unite with people they don't trust.* This fact, combined with the undisputable truth that in our present era people lie like they breathe, unconsciously, means that it is extremely difficult to know who or what to trust.

Consequently, instead of turning outward in our search for satisfaction many turn inward choosing to trust nothing or no one but themselves or that which is familiar. To counter that impulse is where values apply and why it is critical that a person know who they are, what they're about and what they stand for.

If you are as familiar with your values as you are with your name and have meaningful relationships with *only* those that share most of the same values, your chances of being betrayed or victimized are greatly diminished. If you know that your values and theirs are compatible perhaps you can risk bringing them into your circle.

If over time you realize that the actions they take are consistent with the principles they embrace, and that you continue to share those principles, then you can optimistically combine their power with yours and use the combined force to win when you compete.

By knowing others, establishing trust, then combining resources, power exponentially increases. Power that was generated by your ability to trust. Power that can be unleashed by your capacity to believe in someone. External power that is derived from the internal power inside you.

Wherever this place called success is, *you can't get there by yourself.* Somebody else has to show you the way, help you get ready, remove some of the obstacles, provide financing for the trip, offer shelter from the storms you'll encounter, and a place to rest when the journey gets rougher as the going gets tougher.

And even if it were remotely possible to reach success all by yourself, how good would it be to be there all by yourself, with nobody to share it all with or reminisce about the journey, laugh at the highlights or mourn the low points?

When I teach in the classroom, one of my major objectives is maximum engagement by all participants in the cohort. I want my students to grow by being challenged so I often require them to come out of their comfort zone. Nobody gets a chance to sit in the back of the room and hide. Everybody is expected to debate the points, add their input and provide context and content to the topic. Anybody can be called on, or "put on the spot" at any time so everyone remains focused.

One of the primary tactics I use to involve each student and foster a multi-voiced dialogue is through homework writing assignments. The essays are integral to the mix and important to the information flow because they form the basis of the discussion planned for the subsequent class session.

Often, when we reach this portion of my six-week curriculum, I hear groans of apprehension when I announce the writing assignment. "Why is it hard to trust other people," I ask. "Give me two paragraphs and be prepared to read your essay aloud at our next session." Hardly anybody responds with a comment or question, but I can tell by their demeanor and body language (and grumbling) that none are thrilled by this assignment.

Despite their apparent discomfort with the subject, they always deliver, but not two paragraphs. Usually, it's more like two pages; written in small tight letters, crammed on the front, back and margins of the page. A torrent of words from most of them, as if the assignment had unblocked a dam inside them and released the emotional words that described the pain of betrayal and loss; emotions that gushed from them like water from a faucet turned on full.

They write of family members that abused them or siblings who stole from them. They tell of friends who told their secrets, faithless lovers that had affairs, co-workers that took credit for their ideas and bosses who threw them under the bus. They describe stranger-danger on the street or in the neighborhood that causes them to carry weapons and live in homes secured by burglar bars on most of the windows and all of the doors.

Their essays cover multiple horrors. Cousin Betty got swindled out of her house. Uncle Edgar was carjacked at the gas station. Someone's husband cheated with her sister. One man got conned out of his life savings in a phony investment scheme. Somebody's brother is doing life in prison for a crime he didn't commit. An undocumented lady who worked as a nanny experienced sexual abuse from her employer. When she protested the treatment, the man threatened to call I.C.E. if she opened her mouth. Several men's girlfriends were using them as "sugar daddies". Another student turned in a fifteen page essay (no exaggeration). She wrote of being abandoned by her father, physically abused by her step-father, emotionally beat down by her mother and her boyfriend left her for a *man*.

As you can imagine, the pain caused by all of this untrustworthy behavior is immense. The scars left in the wake of the healing serve as constant reminders of the emotional damage done to those whose trust has been betrayed, and a warning that to trust other people is to set yourself up for disappointment, humiliation or harm.

Emotions of anger, grief and embarrassment, combined with self-loathing thoughts like, "I'm such an idiot! How could I be so stupid as to fall for that, or so blind as to not see that? How could I allow that to happen to me," morph into a resolve of *never again*, as in, "I will *never* put myself into a position like that again. I will *never* trust anybody ever again!"

These negative feelings are counterproductive and play directly into the hands of the people who would use every trick imaginable to get rival competitors out of the game. Because none of us can "get there" by ourselves or win by ourselves, not trusting anyone means having almost no chance of getting anywhere at all!

The questions I put to my students after we've examined the emotional carnage and upheaval felt after being betrayed or experiencing someone's treacherous behavior are these: "why should *you* feel stupid, why would you call *yourself* an idiot for *something someone else did to you?* Why should *you* feel diminished or foolish *by another person's* unfaithfulness, disloyalty or other act of betrayal"?

To get to the point I'm trying to make with these questions, I target the biggest, baddest looking dude in my cohort. Walking quickly up to his desk with a fearsome look on my face, I thunder in an aggressive manner, "if I knocked you out of your chair, right now, backhanded you across the face and sent you sprawling, what would you do? How would you feel?"

Stunned by the inanity of my questions and my rapid change in tone, the man hesitates to reply but everybody in the room laughs nervously, knowing full well that the young man, thirty five years younger and fifty pounds heavier, would probably spring to his feet and knock my block off!

To set up the point I'm hoping to make, before he can get words to come from his mouth I say, "you'd probably do any number of things and feel any number of emotions, but self-loathing wouldn't be one of them. You wouldn't feel like an idiot. You wouldn't feel stupid. You might feel anger and probably bewilderment by what I did to you. Most likely you would retaliate in some way, either by physically defending yourself and/or getting me fired.

But I bet you wouldn't feel guilty or diminished because I knocked you out of your chair. I bet you wouldn't blame *yourself* for my behavior, you'd blame *me*. I doubt you would think to yourself," 'I'm never going anywhere ever again because of what Mr. Miller did to me in Empowerment class'.

Having fully captured the attention of every participant in the room, I slow my cadence and lower the volume of my voice to further draw them in as I reveal the lesson behind the Trust Essay assignment.

"We feel stupid or at fault when our trust is broken because we offered something of great value to someone only to have them throw it back in our face. We feel diminished or foolish when we've been victimized because we didn't see it coming. We thought the people who deceived us or tricked us, or had our back were there for us, were in our corner. We thought we were smart enough or street-wise enough to take care of our interests and not be hoodwinked.

But here's the thing, *we didn't do it to ourselves.* Somebody *else* did something to us that hurt us. My young man didn't fall out of the chair, I knocked him out of it. I did that, not him. He's absolutely justified to be angry with me not himself. He's not to blame because I chose to abuse and humiliate him.

When trust is lost however, we blame *ourselves.* We take the pain of betrayal inside us instead of sending it back to the cause. We often feel stupid that we were blind to the motives of others, that we didn't see their true persona and that we left ourselves open to someone who didn't value us like we valued them.

Often we get angry at *ourselves* that we incurred pain caused by *another's* behavior, but the unfortunate fact of the matter is *trust is always at risk when a person is unaware of the other individual's values.*"

For those of you reading this let me bring it back to the here and now. Shared values alone won't stop you from being betrayed. They won't even stop you from having someone try to rip you off. They will however minimize the risk.

To be empowered means to not be a victim. It also means being able to give to others. If you have been victimized by any type of wrong, perpetrated by the actions of any individual it becomes difficult to trust anybody, known or unknown, ever again. But if you don't trust anyone, if everything seems suspicious, then it's almost impossible to be able to give because we won't give to people or institutions that we don't trust.

In the previous chapter I talked about the dichotomy we experience with the need to compete for 'The Four Things', versus our need to have people in our corner willing and able to help us win when we compete. And though it does seem to be a contradiction in terms, it doesn't mean the two ideas are incompatible. What it means is that we have to know who we can trust even though it is inevitable that sometimes those we choose to trust will betray that trust.

The journey of life is filled with uncertainty and risk. Part of the risk comes from trying to work our individual magic and find happiness through other people. Working our magic through other individuals, building relationships with them and working collaborative efforts takes patience, teamwork, loyalty and camaraderie, but it's unlikely that any of those will be possible with people you don't trust.

Society demands truth because societies only succeed on trust. We need to know that the goods are authentic, the service reliable, and the contract will be honored. We want to be sure that promises will be kept, and claims can be verified.

Trust is the *essential* component that makes a society successful. Trust is the glue that binds the social elements, people, institutions, and infrastructure together. Trust is what makes the whole thing function. We need to trust that planes won't fall from the sky, that the bridge we drive over won't collapse, that our food and water are fresh, and that what people say they will do is what they actually will do.

If you can't trust other people then you can't trust the other motorists on the road, the technician who rotates your tires or the dentist that pulls your tooth. If you won't trust people that you have no relationship with then you won't trust the truth when you hear it.

If you refuse to trust people you don't know well then you've got to distrust the baker's bread, the doctor's meds and even what the teacher said. In fact, if you refuse to trust in other folks you'd be better off just staying in bed!

People with a mindset of distrust will likely never become personally empowered because trust *equals* power. Since there's little we can accomplish without the support or affirmation of other people we must embrace their help. This collective trust adds to our individual power. A key concept to incorporate is something I call 'The Power Equation': *No Trust Equals No Unity, No Unity Equals No Strength, No Strength Equals No Protection, No Protection Equals No Power.*

Unity is what produces the power in numbers, but it is the power in you that produces unity. The brilliance unleashed by an individual's curiosity, combined with an open mindset, draws people to them like the salmon attracts the grizzly, which provides a wide swath of diverse individuals with like-minded interests. A test of their values compatibility yields a potential ally. These allies become friends and supporters, the people to rely on for assistance, when (if) you learn that they can be trusted.

Trust begins with candid communication and grows through frequent dialogue and interaction with other individuals. The communication process is two-way, a conversation, not a lecture. The objective of the process is to determine similarities and differences in point of view to develop links or build bridges for the achievement of a shared objective.

For trust to blossom, the conversation must be candid, open and complete. Secrets, hidden agendas, false motives and half-truths will derail the trust building process like an ice encased track will derail a freight train.

Trust is slow to build but can quickly be lost. Trust more often than not, is never taken away by the giver. On the contrary, it is lost by the behavior of the recipient of that trust. Once trust erodes it is almost never regained, but if it is fully reciprocated trust can move mountains.

Unity is all about bringing disparate people together as a committed group and keeping them together to achieve a particular set of objectives. Unity centers on the accomplishment of a specified goal, the successful completion of a group objective or the desired outcome of a team effort. Unity forges power and affords protection by creating strength in numbers, resources and commitment.

Unity is the 'hoist' which provides the uplift and support, the boost, and to a certain degree the protection for the group members. Then it uses that support to further bond the association together. Without trust there is no boost. Eliminate trust and there is no uplift, no support.

Trust and unity development demands a demonstrated commitment over an extended period of time. They require continuous give and take, a sort of 'checking in' to ensure that all are still focused on the specific goal and are comfortable with their role in helping to achieve it.

Unity and trust building share a total need for transparent honesty. To build trust that will last, never forget that your word is your bond. Do what you say you will do when you say you will do it. Be where you say you will be when you say you will be there.

To be empowered means to walk without fear. The strength and power supplied by a trusted network of people that share values helps to lift courage high. That courage can then be used like a massive shield to hold back fear, and a mighty tool to help them win when they compete.

CHAPTER FOURTEEN

'THE 3 C'S' WILL SOLVE THE PROBLEM

When people come together based on any attraction not centered on shared values conflict is sure to result. Perhaps more impactful, when people choose to partner with individuals based on any criteria other than shared values, trust will be difficult to establish and almost impossible to sustain. When the inevitable conflict arises chances to resolve it will be diminished because distrust erects barriers to compromise, a key component to successful conflict resolution.

A conflict is a fight or a struggle. The fight or the struggle is the result of a disagreement, or a misunderstanding. People that hold different values are bound to disagree. People *will* misunderstand the motives or question the behavior of individuals whose actions, language or attitude are driven by a value system they themselves do not embrace.

Think about it. If someone values honesty and a different someone values deception, you can bet the ranch that their relationship will be filled with disagreements or distrust. If one spouse values loyalty and the other is unfaithful, a misunderstanding or disagreement is the least that can be expected.

Should you find yourself as the hard working business partner of individuals who are lazy, don't pull their weight or lack integrity, disagreements and misunderstandings will likely sink the enterprise or cause you to quit. If one believes living below their means and saving for the future is important while their significant other burns through cash and maxes out credit like there's 'no tomorrow', disagreements will be their constant, and conflict will continuously loom.

Trust, as discussed in chapter thirteen, demands truth. The truth is often a casualty of disagreements or misunderstandings because a person's tendency is to lie, either by commission or omission, to forestall an argument or to not provoke a reaction that will lead to a fractured relationship or all-out war.

All-out war, physical retaliation, or a make them pay mentality often results from unresolved conflict but should be used as measures of last resort because the fallout from the conflict will likely remove an individual from the competitive arena and will usually end in failure to achieve 'The Four Things'.

Many people try to *avoid* conflict by staying away from locations and situations that make them uncomfortable. They *avoid* individuals whose customs, culture or points of view they misunderstand. Some try to *ignore* conflict choosing to act like the conflict isn't happening or doesn't involve them. A few individuals deliberately *cause* conflict hoping to profit from the disruption their actions provoked.

Still more *flee* conflict. They run from it when they see it coming or try to escape it if it somehow engulfs them. Some *confront* it; boldly standing ground in the face of the argument caused by the disagreement or misunderstanding, refusing to be swayed from their position no matter what. A few deal with conflict by *blaming* the cause on the other side or the other person, refusing to see their own culpability in the dispute.

None of those tactics are effective however because even though it's possible to run, it's not possible to hide. In a world of almost eight billion souls, most trying to do the exact same four things, disagreements and misunderstandings are as constant as the North Star. Conflict will find you, and when it does, in order to win when you compete you can't let it overwhelm you or remove you from the game.

A better strategy is to minimize the opportunities for conflict by partnering with and trusting only those that share your values. Since that's not always possible, (because we're often attracted to people for numerous reasons other than their values) actively resolving the potential conflict by sorting out the disagreement or clearing up the misunderstanding is the tactic to utilize.

You've got to resolve it, not avoid it. Resolve it, not ignore it. Resolve it, not flee from it or hide from it. Resolve it, not point your finger at the other side. Resolve it, by using the Three C's of Conflict Resolution: *Communication*, *Consensus* and *Compromise*.

To be empowered means *to be able to communicate effectively*. Something that is effective, is something that works. For communication to work for you means having the ability to let other individuals know what you need in the hope that they will be interested in helping you get it.

To communicate is to make something known. Communication is the transmission of news and information to and fro or back and forth. Its purpose is to pass knowledge and input to other people, have social interaction with them, determine their value system, and gather insight on their personality, point of view, motives and behavior.

Most people who've participated in my Program, when asked to list the ways humans communicate with each other, always put talk at the top. Rarely do they include the word listen anywhere on the list.

A newborn child, unable to talk, nonetheless communicates with its mother or caregiver. Using cries, facial expressions, and body language the infant lets the people it depends on for survival know exactly what it needs. Cries to inform of hunger. Cries, grimaces and fitfulness to pass the news that it is sick or teething. Cries and uncomfortable squirming when its diaper needs changing. Giggles, shining eyes, babbling and sighs of contentment when it's at peace.

The newborn's parents must stay attentive and remain engaged to decipher the communication correctly. They must become attuned to each of their baby's communication methods to insure that the right need is immediately addressed.

Human beings grow and change as they age of course, but the primary reason for communication does not. From our beginning to our end, we communicate first and foremost to let other people know what we need. Part of the angst experienced by so many of our contemporaries it seems to me, is that with all the crying people do, cries for fairness, cries for diversity, equality and shared prosperity, cries for freedom and justice, nobody appears to be listening.

Effective communication incorporates a variety of methods to transmit information. People talk to each other and employ different vocal tones to convey emotion. They use and interpret body language, facial expressions, gestures and non-verbal cues. They read print, sign language and braille.

However, if people talk but fail to listen, if they read but fail to write, if they misinterpret someone's body language then the correct, accurate, factual information cannot be passed to and fro. It doesn't go back and forth so the communication process is ineffective. This ineffective attempt to communicate will then produce the type of disagreements or misunderstandings that if not resolved will lead to conflict.

In many cases ineffective communication will not only lead to conflict, it will also heighten the risk that conflict will spiral out of control. To lessen that risk ineffective must be transformed to effective to trigger *consensus*, the second stage of the conflict resolution process.

For a misunderstanding to be cleared up or a disagreement patched up both parties have to agree that they want it to happen. This agreement, or consensus, allows the opportunity to move toward the third stage of conflict resolution, *compromise*.

But if one of the parties doesn't wish to form consensus, should they not want to agree that clearing up the dispute is worth it, or is of value to them, then compromise is unlikely. Without the give and take of compromise it will be difficult to resolve the conflict satisfactorily, yet without trust compromise itself is a non-starter.

Occasionally, when explaining this concept to my students some of them are not clear on the point I'm trying to make in discussing this third stage of conflict resolution. To them, compromise has always meant being put into a situation not of their choosing, being exploited after being exposed in an unflattering light or having been taken advantage of in some way.

So, let me be clear. To resolve conflict successfully neither party should be left feeling that they got punked or played like a chump. Rather than feeling like a dupe or a sucker or someone who had to take the short end of the stick, compromise as relates to conflict resolution should be a win-win for both sides.

I listen to your point of view; you listen to mine. I give something to satisfy you or make amends, you give me something that does the same. Then we both walk away feeling that our needs were met, our position was validated and that we didn't get played like a fiddle.

Without trust none of that will happen. The lack of trust creates barriers, not bridges, and compromise is a bridge to peace. Effective communication creates the piles that support the bridge of compromise. Effective communication is the girder that reinforces all the main beams of the bridge, including trust. Effective communication is the deck of the bridge that provides a pathway to consensus.

Often when I ask my younger cohorts to list the ways human beings communicate with each other they misread my question because of its vagueness. They don't list talk, listen, read, write, sign language, body language, facial expressions, gestures, tone or eye movements. Instead, they list phone, text, instant messaging, TV, Facebook, Instagram and other social media platforms and apps.

And although some of the communication devices my students list pass news and information back and forth none of them are capable of resolving conflict. None lead to consensus. None bring about compromise.

A communication device is not a communication method. A newspaper or magazine transmits news, advertisements and information but it only goes one way primarily, from the publisher to the reader. Television shows, radio programming and podcasts essentially work the same way (though all these mediums try to foster two way communication through letters to the editor, opinion call-ins and their social media sites with limited results).

Social Media comes closest to pure communication because of the back and forth nature of the medium and the opportunity to like, comment or review, yet a vast number of social media consumers use the platforms to post or view videos that provide few options for real time two-way feedback on input received.

Texts, instant messages and emails once written have to be read. Once read they call for a response. "Did you get my message? Did you get my text? Did you read my email," are questions asked thousands of time every day.

With the possible exceptions of television and radio programming, all of these devices and communication mediums can be used to determine if consensus can be reached. Some of them can be utilized to pass information back and forth. None of them can be used to engender compromise though because compromise demands trust and trust, as discussed in chapter thirteen, takes time to build.

To successfully transform ineffective communication to effective communication and resolve conflict with the people you need and want to remain in you circle of support, face to face is best. Face to face you can read body language, facial expressions and gestures. Face to face you can talk, look them in the eye, and gauge reaction to what was said.

Face to face you can listen as the other person replies and respond to their position on the spot. Face to face you can ascertain and display sincerity and credibility. Face to face both parties can quickly agree to resolve the misunderstanding or determine the steps to take to do so.

Face to face you can readily find areas of give and take. Face to face both sides can improve their relationship and strengthen it by using the disagreement as a learning experience or the cleared up misunderstanding as a way to fortify their bond.

One of the things being empowered means is *not having to look over your shoulder.* Looking over your shoulder indicates that you think that somebody is coming for you, somebody who thinks you did them wrong. Looking over your shoulder is a tacit acknowledgement that a disagreement, a misunderstanding or a failure to keep your word has unleashed a force that demands retribution.

Avoided conflict, ignored conflict, and defiantly confronted conflict will haunt and cause problems throughout life's journey if not resolved. Fled-from conflict and deliberately provoked conflict will ultimately catch or trip you up due to the phenomenon of karma.

To win when you compete you've got to keep it moving forward. To maintain the strong team of supporters every successful competitor needs means keeping them motivated to push you. You can't move forward with confidence if you're looking behind you to see what's coming for you. And you won't keep your team motivated and in your corner if you can't resolve misunderstandings or disagreements before they lead to disruptions that will stop your forward momentum.

CHAPTER FIFTEEN

A DIFFERENT PERSPECTIVE ON GOALS AND OBJECTIVES

To maintain your life journey's momentum while keeping it moving forward means you have to know where you're going and have a darn good idea of how to get there. Uncertainty as to the route to take will cause delays, detours and unnecessary setbacks. Regardless of the path you choose to get to where you plan to go, to make the trip successfully means you'll have to incorporate two separate yet interwoven strategies and use them as your guide, strategies that are often mistaken one for the other.

Every profession under the sun, every entrepreneurial endeavor and every life calling from the letter A to the letter Z has to set *objectives* and meet *goals*. Invariably, English speaking people I've worked with in every field I've worked confuse these two words, or even worse think they can be used interchangeably like synonyms.

I say even worse because one of the reasons so many fail to achieve *'The Four Things'* and are bewildered as to why they can't accomplish what others can is because they don't know the difference between objectives and goals. Consequently, when they fail and try again they fail again, which means that they will ultimately quit or "*settle*" because that's what happens when life's failures outweigh life's successes.

Objectives and goals are not synonyms. An objective is the *End Game* the place one is ultimately trying to reach. Goals are the steps to take to reach that objective. Goals are markers, measuring sticks and signposts to chart progress and keep one on track to the *End Game*.

I frequently get pushback from students and colleagues when I broach this concept. Sometimes, believe it or not, they actually become incensed with me, irately insisting that it's just the opposite, or that a goal is the end game, and an objective is too! When I ask them what they plan to do to reach the end game of their choice they usually just stare back at me with a look that says, 'what are you talking about'? If I've confused you too, let me provide clarity by offering a sports analogy.

If you're familiar with the game of American football, you know that it's played from the Pee Wee leagues to the Pro leagues. It's played in high school and college, in intramural leagues and pick-up games at the park, in the backyard or even in the street. There's flag football, two-hand touch, tackle football, and in some neighborhoods, with not enough kids to block for the quarterback, the opposing player has to count to 5-Mississippi before they can rush him.

All football teams are not created equal nor do the players on the different types of teams have the same talent, coaching or skill level. *They all have the same end game though.* From Pee Wee to the street, to high school, college and the pros, *they all want to win.* Because of the differing skills or the various talents the players bring to the game, each team, with the same objective of winning sets their goals, the steps they plan to take to reach the objective: score more points than the opposing team and win the game.

A team with a laser armed quarterback and fleet footed receivers might set goals of passing for yardage to help them win. A team equipped with quicksilver running backs and blockers who can clear a path for them may set goals of running for first downs to win. A team with a weak offense but strong defense will likely set goals of stopping the pass, limiting the run and denying first downs to help them win. A team with a "can't miss" kicker will set a goal of getting within field goal range every time their offense controls the ball.

Football teams set all kinds of goals. Goals of managing the clock, conserving time outs and how often to call for the run or the pass. They set goals for their special teams, kicking teams, and management teams. Win or lose at the end of the day each team's management will review the outcome through an assessment of goal attainment. If they met their goals and won the game they'll probably keep doing what they did to come out on top. If they met their goals but lost the game they'll likely modify their goal strategy.

No team however will ever change their objective. No team will ever change their endgame of winning. Instead they'll tweak the steps they need to take, the goals they need to set, to help them win the next one.

An objective is the purpose behind the action, the reason for doing the activity. The action is determined by the goals that are set, which indicate the steps to take to achieve the desired outcome. As relates to 'The Four Things' almost everybody on the planet is trying to do, the objective is to attain. The *End Game* is to succeed through the accomplishment of the deeds necessary to obtain, maintain and sustain. Each of the three in actuality is a goal that must be met in order to attain.

One of the reasons I think American Football is so popular with so many different people is that it reflects a great deal of real life. Uncertainty, swagger, suspense, violence. Arduous competition with clearly defined winners and losers. Setbacks off-set by forward momentum. Bruising and pain. Comebacks, heroes and scapegoats. Intense satisfaction when it goes your team's way, despondence and despair when it doesn't. The bitter pill of defeat. The sweet taste of success.

Success for the vast majority of us is the *End Game* but unfortunately the vast majority doesn't get to taste it. In fact far too many individuals will never taste it, they'll only know the lingering aftertaste of failure because they mistake the goals (obtain, maintain, sustain) for the *End Game*.

Some of us think that success comes in the getting so they spend time, money and energy acquiring things and toys. Other people presume that success comes from their capability to keep what they were able to get so they hoard, refuse to share and doubt the motives of people. Certain folks believe that increasing what they've been able to keep is the mark of a successful individual, so they become greedy or socially indifferent.

Many of the people who've become consumed by chasing their particular version of success fail to recognize that they won't catch it. On the contrary they're actively setting themselves up for failure because in life, unlike a football game, the goalposts keep moving as more and more people enter the competitive arena and try to re-define the meaning of winning, of success.

The old saying, "nothing beats a failure but a try" is actually a variation of the motivational phrase we learned as children, "if at first you don't succeed try, try again." Both sayings illustrate what far too many of our fellow citizens have never been taught (or if they were media messages have altered their perception), *success is not what you own, success is what you do.*

Success is not a noun. Success is a verb! You *do* success and since (as we discussed in chapter two) behavior is also what you do it is your behavior that will determine whether you succeed in life or whether you fail.

Somewhere along the way our society lost that idea. Somewhere in time, "if at first you don't succeed try, try again" became 'if at first you don't succeed the hell with it, try something else'. Somehow, instant gratification (we want the world, and we want it now) became the tenor of our times, and somehow *success is what you do* has changed to success is what you have; how much prestige you have, how much net worth you have, the type of vehicle you drive, how many toys you own, how big your house is and what zip code it's located in.

And though the misleading definition of the meaning of success as the accumulation of riches has taken hold in most of the U.S. and much of the Western world, it is a false notion because success is not what you own, success is what you do. *Success is the ability to influence the thoughts, actions and ideas of other people by what you do.* Should you doubt that assertion or question my definition, consider the exercise I often conduct with my students to explain my concept of success and clearly illustrate it's veracity.

"Think of a person that you consider to be a success," I ask them. "It can be anyone in any country, living or dead, male or female, young or old. Let's fill up this whiteboard with their names, then we'll talk about why you chose them."

After a brief hesitation to mentally absorb the assignment and seize on a candidate, the answers come flooding in; a cascade of names as my students, their voices rising in excitement, enthusiastically respond to the question and in so doing make my point for me.

"Maya Angelou, Jeff Bezos, My Mother, Michael Jordan, Michael Jackson, Father Thomas, Tyler Perry, my Uncle Tony, Bill Gates, Martin Luther King Jr., Oprah, Tupac, Warren Buffett, Mrs. Hoffman, Thurgood Marshall, Michelle Obama, Richard Pryor, Steve Jobs, Susan B. Anthony, Barack Obama, Bubba Smith, Pastor Wilson, Beyonce, Spike Lee, Jay-Z, Simone Biles, my Big Brother, Steve Jobs, Will Smith, Wynton Marsalis, my Sister, Frederick Douglass, Me, Mr. Miller, my Father, Tom Brady, Trevor Noah, Tyra Banks."

The insight provided through all these responses is remarkable. Not only by the diversity of the candidates chosen but, as further dialogue on the topic revealed, the reason for the choices.

"My mother raised seven kids all by herself," said one young woman when I asked why she included her mom on the successful people list. "She worked two jobs, six days a week but she never missed a school event or failed to protect us. She was never too tired, always had time for us and made each of us feel special. I want to be just like her when I have my own family."

"Bill Gates cornered the PC market with his Microsoft software," someone said. "He kept improving his product till he had the majority of the business. That's why I'm studying Coding. If he could do it maybe I can too."

"Michael Jackson was it! The way he moved, the way he danced, the way he dressed, the way he sang was...I can't even put it into words! All I know is I imitated his every move! For a minute there, before my voice changed I could sound just like him. Got into some talent shows and felt really good about myself"!

"Father Thomas was the Principal of my elementary school but also someone the whole neighborhood relied on. You could always go to him for help. He didn't look down on anybody. If they needed food, help with the bills or someplace to live Father Thomas was there. He had our back. I watched how he operated and now that I'm grown I try to be the same way."

"When I played basketball I wanted to play like Mike. I had to float from the free throw line, stick my tongue out, tried to drive the lane and throw down a monster dunk! I had Jordan's shoes, his jersey and always wore number 23. Michael was a leader and knew how to make his teammates better. He knew how to win"!

"Mrs. Hoffman was the neighbor down the street. She had a big garden, flowers everywhere. She always gave away vegetables to anybody who asked for some, wouldn't take any money for them, can you believe that? Her flowers were so pretty, made the whole block look important. She taught me so much."

"I chose Tupac because his lyrics inspire me like poetry you know? His delivery, the way he put the words together with power and force made me want to listen to what he had to say. I found a lot of truth in Tupac."

"Jeff Bezos because he created an on-line bookselling operation and grew it into a massive retail conglomerate that changed everything about the way the world buys, sells and ships consumer products."

On and on it went. One success comment feeding into another. No one explained their success choice as having been picked for their fame, celebrity or what they had acquired. Each one justified their choice by what the individual had done to *make things better* or how they inspired or influenced other people to do or think or live.

The things individual success brings, the financial rewards, the perks and privileges that media portrays as the quintessential trappings of success, are simply byproducts of the extraordinary work and relentless effort people put in to achieve it. Influence the thoughts, actions or ideas of large numbers of people and usually the dollars will flow, and the honors will follow.

Highly influential people like Oprah, the Obamas, Michael Jordan or the Kardashians are paid huge dollars to influence their followers who look up to them and will heed their advice.

People with huge impact like Bezos, Buffett, Gates, Jay-Z and Jobs (Apple) make huge money because their ideas and innovations have been embraced by so many.

Entertainers like Tom Brady, Michael Jackson, Tyler Perry, Will Smith, Tiger Woods and Beyonce command top dollar and have acquired great wealth because their talent and work ethic draws millions of people to them.

Thought leaders like Maya Angelou, Mahatma Ghandi, Martin Luther King Jr., Thurgood Marshall, Mother Theresa or Malcolm X never got rich or lived in a mansion or drove a luxury car. Yet they're atop the success list because they influenced change and inspired generations of people. They're on the list not because of what they had but what they did.

It was the students that included their relatives on the list though, that best personifies the meaning of success. The one's that told the class about what their sister showed them, what their brother taught them, what their father gave them, and what it meant to their development to have an aunt or uncle to influence them or parents that sacrificed so that they could grow and thrive.

To succeed throughout every step of your life's journey is not an impossible task. On the contrary it is relatively easy. All you have to do, is do your talent. Do it consistently, do it repeatedly, do it persistently with an eye on your objective, your *End Game* and a focus on your goals, the steps you must take to reach that objective. To make that happen you'll need a plan to drive the action.

CHAPTER SIXTEEN

THE SEVEN POINT ACTION PLAN

When I was thirty seven I quit my lucrative career in Sales Management to venture out on my own. I'd grown dissatisfied with the non-stop effort to meet corporate sales goals and working with a customer base whose bigoted views indicated that though I might get close to the glass ceiling, cracking it to get to the big money top, would probably happen only in my dreams.

I was just starting to learn much of what I'm sharing with you in this book, particularly about purpose and talent. I had come to suspect that my God-given purpose was not to sell food products, consumer goods or business technology tools for blue chip companies, and I was more interested in using my God-given talents to make a difference in the world, while making money to sustain my family instead of my bosses.

So, taking a huge leap of faith (and with little understanding of the enormity of the journey I was embarking on) I left the world of steady paychecks, corporate perks, bonuses and stock options to try to control my own destiny. I was on a quest to Max-My-Po (even though I didn't yet know that), succeed or fail on my own merits and find professional satisfaction as the owner of a company whose direction I would set.

In the beginning, as I was chasing dollars to help start my TV production company, Jammin II Incorporated, everybody was telling me that I needed a Business Plan to have any chance of attracting investment capital, securing a bank loan or acquiring a business partner to share the financial load.

Simultaneous to receiving this advice, the television people I reached out to, the consultants, experts, and broadcast professionals were all telling me that I would need a Marketing Plan. A strategy detailing how I was going to distribute my programming, how I planned to promote the content, what I'd use to attract viewers and my methods to build an audience large enough to receive advertising revenue. A business plan combined with a marketing plan they all advised was the way to go. They further cautioned, no one would take me seriously without both documents.

So I drafted and crafted plans. In fact, I put together so many variations of business and marketing plans for so many different entities that I began to think that these plans were just another way to limit the field by keeping people out of the entrepreneurial game!

The plans were comprehensive and intense. The business plan involved everything from the type of corporate entity, to who would comprise the Board of Directors, what their compensation would be and profit projections for years one through five. It included projecting costs for the physical plant, number of employees, their compensation and duties, number of corporate officers, operating equipment, fixed costs vs. variable costs and how the investors would share in the profits.

The marketing plan was constantly in flux as the concept I was building continued to evolve. Since there were so many unknowns at this stage of my venture, the marketing plan became a document of hopes as opposed to a document that set the direction, the objectives and the goals for my creative enterprise.

In actuality both of these documents took considerable time and effort to produce but contributed little to the success of my endeavor because they were based on assumptions, if comes and "Blue Sky" projections. After a succession of "no thanks", "not interested", or "call me back in six months" I realized that I'd have to get the bandwagon rolling by myself before others came to jump on.

What I needed I figured, was to create a different type of plan, not a business plan or a marketing plan but a personal plan to make my personal dreams real. I needed a simple one-page plan to not only drive my action but guide it. My *Seven Point Action Plan* is the result of that thought.

As discussed in chapter two, your individual plan, the fourth essential element to Max-Yo-Po will provide the blueprint, roadmap and the "how-to" guide to follow in your objective to reach that place called success. For a plan to be successful though it must be written down because a plan that is not written down, that is just floating around in your mind is only an idea; an idea that will be pushed out of your head or moved to the back of your consciousness when the next big idea comes to mind.

The *Seven Point Action Plan* is a written document to refer to, revise, and use to chart your progress. It serves as a step-by-step manual on how to achieve the objective you have set. Your plan tells you what you need to do and when you need to do it to drive your action.

Anything you want to do and everything you need to do can be accomplished with this plan and by following each step in sequential order. Once you've locked the format in and begin to work the process, it adapts to any objective you choose to set. *End Games* like obtaining a house, degree, car or other possessions of value. Moving out of your parent's house. Becoming a parent yourself. Getting a raise or a promotion. Traveling the world. Becoming an entrepreneur. Raising a garden. Learning a new skill.

Take a minute to think about your Big Dream, your God-given talent and your wish list for your future. Keep those things top of mind as I lay out the points covered in this action plan. Most of us have a wish list or two. Many of us have big dreams and all of us have our special gift(s). Yet far too many are unable to use those talents to fulfill their wish list or realize their dreams because *they don't know how or where to start.* Which means they can't see the *End Game*, or even what steps to take to reach it.

These people likely won't meet their objective because they lack a plan of attack, but since you're reading this book you'll now have the advantage of an effective planning process that will keep you on track to your end game, and help you win much more often than you lose.

THE SEVEN POINT ACTION PLAN

Number 1, at the top of the list is the **OBJECTIVE.** Whatever it is that you want to do, or need to do, or hope to do goes under this heading. "I want to buy a house; I need to get married; I hope to find a job in IT," etc. This objective must be front and center in your mind's eye *and* on the page. This is your motivating factor. This is what Muhammad Ali and Jesse Jackson were talking about with their variations of Napoleon Hill's 1937 quote, "Whatever your mind can conceive and believe it can achieve." As Ali put it, "If my mind can conceive it and my heart can believe it, then I can achieve it." As previously discussed, the objective is your *End Game*, the place you're ultimately trying to reach.

Number 2 is **TIMELINE**. This point is where would be planners often trip themselves up, but it is essential to the planning process. *When will I do what I say I want to do by...*Under this header is where you put your completion date, your deadline date to meet the objective. "I want to buy a house twelve months from today's date." "I need to get married by the time I'm 28." "I hope to find a job in IT by April 5th."

The **TIMELINE** drives the action. It can't be open ended or span multiple years because that stalls momentum by stifling the urgency to act now. An open ended timeline dulls desire for the objective as life challenges intrude. Without a deadline date to shoot for, "I want to" often turns into "maybe someday," or even the abandonment of the dream itself.

Have you ever known someone who is always talking about the big things they plan to do but never does any of those things? Chances are these individuals never put the timeline, the "by when" date, to the objective. Chances are also good that it is people like these that confuse the idea in their mind for the written plan that will make it come to fruition.

Number 3 of the Seven Point Action Plan is **RESEARCH**. This is the step in which you figure out the how. *How will I do what I say I need to do in the timeframe I need to do it by?* "How do I buy the house I'm interested in twelve months from now"? "How will I find my wife or husband by the time I'm 28"? "How will I find a job in IT by April 5th"?

What steps do I have to take and when do I have to take them to make my objective real? This is an essential point. What you discover during this research or 'how to' phase of the planning process will be integral to the progress you're able to make.

Number 4 on the list is **PRIORITIZE**. Often my students are confused by this item, unsure of just what they're supposed to prioritize. They get the 'do things in order of importance' idea but not the things that they're supposed to do. In the *Seven Point Action Plan*, what one prioritizes is the how, the research findings from point three. Let me give you an example.

Suppose your objective is to get a software development position at an IT company or enroll at the university of your choice. There's a great deal of work to do to make either of those objectives happen. You've got to research the criteria they're looking for and meet the qualifications. You've got to apply and generate interest for your candidacy. There are deadlines to adhere to and documents to submit. In both cases an interview (perhaps multiple) will have to be scheduled which you'll have to Ace to get the position or gain admission to the school. It's likely that you'll need to upgrade your wardrobe, move to a distant location, acquire housing, transportation, cover fees and meet other financial obligations.

To prioritize the how, you determine which of these things must be done before the others can proceed. Which item is the most important to accomplish? Which item can wait? What do you do first, second, third, fourth, etc.?

The items on your priority list become your goals, your steps to take to reach the objective. They become the items that you check off. They are the signposts that indicate you're making progress. As you reduce the items on your priority list and actually see your progression, the ego boost and power surge that results will motivate you to keep it going until you reach the *End Game*.

Number 5 on the *Seven Point Action Plan* list is **Action Steps.** This is the component where you literally and actively do the things that you learned were necessary in your research. Prepare the resume. Get the transcripts, Make the phone calls. Send out the letters. Develop all the material you need to reach each goal on the priority list. Network, take classes, practice interview. Action steps is where you set yourself up to win by diligently completing each task indicated by your priorities.

Now to do all of this and at the same time keep the other parts of your life rolling means that you're going to be extremely busy satisfying all your obligations. There's going to be a lot of moving parts and you can't afford to forget anything, or miss something, or mess everything up. To maintain focus and commitment to your objective you'll need a tool to help. That tool is the next step of the *Seven Point Action Plan.*

Number 6 is **Daily To Do Lists**. A daily list of all the things you must accomplish in the next twenty four hours to further your goals, get closer to your objective, handle your normal obligations and fulfill personal desires.

Perhaps you need to do online banking or stop by a bank branch to handle some business. Maybe you want to attend your child's school function, go to the dry cleaners, do the laundry, go on a date or visit a relative. Conceivably you have work or school responsibilities, have to pay some bills, maintain your house, or shop for groceries and consumer goods.

At the same time you're working on the goals set by your priorities. You're contacting employers, seeking financing, developing presentations, assembling documents. You're making phone calls, sending emails, going to seminars and attending meetings.

All of these things need to be done using your "A" game and it seems, the more you do the more you have to do. The beauty of the daily to do list is not only in what it offers as a way to minimize forgetfulness or stress but also as a source of motivation and satisfaction. At the end of the day as you compose your **To Do List** for tomorrow's activity you'll be able to clearly see what was accomplished and what remains to be completed. You'll get a jolt of positive self-esteem as you check "done" on key items, which will provide the internal desire to keep it moving forward.

Whatever doesn't get accomplished rolls over to the following day and with consistent effort everything you need to do to reach your goals and meet the objective will have been achieved. An added benefit is that the **Daily To Do Lists** provide a record of what was done and when, what methods were used, who was instrumental to the achievement and contact information of people or institutions that can be accessed later or added to a database.

Should you find that an item has not been completed thirty days after it was first included on the list, chances are that it's either not necessary to your success or something that you'd rather avoid. If it's the former then delete it, but if it's the latter it must be addressed because, "no guts, no glory."

All six of these components are essential to the plan's success and each must be performed in sequential order, but it is point number seven that will have the greatest impact on the success or failure of any action plan you or I will ever conceive.

Number 7 on the list is **Review, Revise, Refine**. Plans don't always work as conceived especially when they're first implemented. Sometimes something was incorrectly assumed. Sometimes something goes wrong or is misunderstood. Sometimes somebody drops the ball. Sometimes people work the plan steps out of sequence. Sometimes the **TIMELINE** isn't realistic to the **OBJECTIVE**. Sometimes the objective is more difficult than originally thought which will cause a delay to the timeline or the need to re-order the **PRIORITIES**.

But if something goes wrong in the plan, if the plan doesn't work immediately, the impulse to discard the plan, crumple it up in disgust, or blow it up and start over must be resisted. Instead the plan should be **reviewed** to try to discern why it isn't working. Each of the six components needs to be carefully examined to determine if the activity called for in that step was completed properly. Special attention should be given to the timeline, priorities, and action steps and include a review of the daily to do lists to make sure the T's were crossed and I's dotted.

If the objective is real and true to you, if it is something that you definitely need or want do, if you actually believe that it's doable based on your *Purpose* and *Talent* then you never throw your plan out. Rather, you **revise** it by making the necessary changes revealed through your review. You tweak it, fine tune it, slightly modify it, and in so doing you make it better, you **refine** it.

Let me illuminate the point I'm trying to make by sharing a brief personal story. When I decided to leave corporate life to become a media entrepreneur, I wanted to produce television programming that would change the negative media image of people classified as Black in America. The initial idea was to pitch a show to the TV Networks, but I decided to go bigger and form a company that would not only produce the content but also distribute it.

The flagship program of my venture was to be a program called **TRANSITION**, my initial foray into weekly TV programming. We ultimately produced more than 320 episodes of that show, won a couple of Broadcast Emmys and CableACE Awards and garnered an audience in the millions, but that's not why I'm telling you this story.

When I first set out, I didn't have a simple plan. I hadn't yet developed the *Seven Point Action Plan* I'm laying out for you here and chose to start with little more than a few assumptions. I had nothing written down except a few notes on a yellow pad. I had no clear path to follow.

I knew I needed to form a business entity to get started and I knew I needed some money to help fund it, but I didn't yet know what type of company to establish or how to go about it. So I engaged some lawyers and financial advisors, formed a corporation, printed shares of stock and filed my paperwork with the State.

My counsellors advised that I would need a business plan to attract the financial angels or institutional investors to provide seed capital and, if I was interested in loans, something to show the banks. As mentioned earlier in this chapter, I spent considerable time on that effort.

Initially I had said to myself that I wanted to be on the air with my programming eighteen months from my start-up date. My objective and timeline were clear but that was about it. So I went out and started to chase all this capital I thought I needed. Every meeting I had with prospects I supposed had the money or interest to invest, despite all the inducements I would offer regarding return on investment and the typical financial promises, all ended with questions I couldn't yet answer.

"Well, what's the show about"? What Network will it air on"? "Do you have a time period for the show yet"? "What advertisers do you have lined up"? "Who's the star"? "Do you have something I can see; do you have a demo"?

What they were really asking was 'does this guy know what he's doing? Is he for real? Can I trust him'? Because I couldn't answer those questions yet, I remember feeling like a fool.

After a couple months of this, growing discouraged I started to think, 'this is ridiculous. I'm never going to make my timeline of eighteen months at this rate. Maybe this TV thing is a dumbass idea.' But ... I wanted to do it. I thought I was capable of doing it and I wasn't ready to quit. So then I thought, 'let me look at this thing, let me find out what's wrong here'. AND THEN I SAW IT. My priorities were out of whack!

I assumed I needed to go chase and catch the money first but what I really needed first was a product, something tangible that could be seen or felt. I needed to be able to show folks what I had. I needed TV stations or a network to buy-in before an investor, a sponsor or an advertiser would. I needed an exciting promotional packet that vividly illustrated the opportunity I was offering before I could ask anybody for anything.

So I revised my thinking and re-ordered my priorities. I contracted a television production company, wrote the pilot program, taped a couple of demo episodes, and used them to sell the concept, secure a distribution deal and lock in my first sponsor.

I didn't get an infusion of cash from the investors. Initially I had to use my own money; sold my stocks, my rings, my bling and expensive things, then lived on starvation rations for a minute until we got it rolling. The people who loved me also assisted with their time, talent and money to get me over the hump.

But I did not abandon the plan. The plan that provided a sixteen year on-air career and gave me a chance to make a difference. The plan that led to my first book, '*Up From the Under, What We Should Do Next*', which led to '*The Empowerment Project with Jeffrey Miller*', and to me talking to you now.

I didn't throw out my plan. I reviewed it to find its flaws, revised it to make it work and in the process I was able to refine it, to make it better.

CHAPTER SEVENTEEN

THE 4-C'S:
AN UNSTOPPABLE FORCE

Once you've put it all together, once you've added the knowledge and power provided by the twelve 'Empowerment Principles' to the four elements to maximize potential (*Mindset, Behavior, Action Steps Individual Planning*), you will be a formidable competitor every time you step into the arena.

If your mindset is right, and by right I mean open, optimistic and actively engaged, it will positively impact your behavior, what you do, and heavily influence your action, the steps you take to win. When you plan those steps through your seven point action plan, and actively work the plan, your odds of reaching your objective will provide an awesome competitive advantage when you try to achieve the four things almost everybody on the planet is trying to do.

When you're personally empowered and can control fear by using courage as a shield, when you're able to communicate effectively to let other people know what you need, when you're capable of diffusing or resolving conflict by using all of your communication skills to find consensus and agree to compromise, you will possess the confidence and display a competence that other people competing in life's arena will find hard to match.

As you work your talent to discover your purpose, as you live your values and learn who or how to trust, while you set objectives and reach the goals that will lead successfully to your end game, your skill-set will become intimidating to those unable to keep up.

After you've avoided the traps meant to take or keep you out of the game and ignored the dream stealers discouragement, your self-esteem will be enormous, your attitude tremendous and your ability to win consistently when you compete will be enhanced.

When you use the interest stimulated by your curiosity to become *Super-Literate* and utilize your curiosity to unleash your brilliance you'll quickly discern lies from truth.

Should you incorporate my *Treasure Map*, the 'Sixteen 'P's' to Success', you'll travel from Curiosity's door, through Personal Empowerment, to Maximized Potential and eventually arrive at Self-Actualization. Once there you'll be remarkably close to the top of your game, but to become an *unstoppable force* when you compete you'll need to possess and continuously showcase each of the 4-C's: *Capability, Credibility, Credentials* and *Character*.

People that win consistently often use superior talent, skill or experience to outdo the opponent. They use endurance, conditioning and practice to hone their performance, remain razor sharp and able to withstand or overcome the effort of those they compete against.

One of the major tactics consistent winners use is to "psyche out" or intimidate the competition before the game begins. Their reputation, their prowess and their personality precedes them into the arena. The force provided by these intangible strengths is often enough to lessen the confidence of those who would compete against them. It provides an edge to the consistent winner that when coupled with superior play will usually result in victory, frequently delivered as a knock-out punch.

The 4-C's are that force. The 4-C's deliver that type of hit. The 4-C's establish the reputation and help form the personality of the consistent winner. The 4-C's are the intangibles that will help you win much more than you lose.

Add these 4-C's to the Self-Actualized state of mind I mentioned in the preceding paragraphs of this chapter and employ them as part of the courage shield you wield to hold back fear. If you do, the impact they will have on your competitive effort to achieve 'The Four Things' will be enormous and your resulting attainment overwhelming.

THE 4 C's

1. CAPABILITY

To be capable is to be able, able to do it. When you're capable you *know*. You're not learning, or training, experimenting, or trying. What a person is capable of is what they are confident of being able to do. They know how. They've done it countless times before. They've done it deliberately, done it instinctively, done it meticulously, to the point of unconscious competence. Other people have seen them do it and know as they say, "what they are capable of".

When someone has a capability they become self-assured, self-reliant and positive about what they set out to do. They radiate assertiveness and a certainty of what they're about, which makes them intimidating to others who would compete against them.

Capability is why it is so important to work your special gift, your God-given talent. It's much easier to master something that you love or desire to do. It's much more rewarding to earn your daily bread or succeed in life by doing the things inspired by your talent.

2. CREDIBILITY

To be credible is to be believable based upon the truth of a person's words or current and past actions. Credibility is sometimes a strange thing because unlike capability, credibility is often bestowed on a person without merit or reason centered on someone else's perception of that individual's power position.

Capability is cut and dried, either you can do it, or you can't. Credibility is similar to capability in the fact that both attributes must be seen or experienced to be believed, but with capability the strength lies in the individual's personal knowledge of what he or she can do.

Although an empowering individual trait, credibility on the other hand is grounded in how truthful a person is perceived to be by *other* people. Some professions and the individuals who choose them are alleged to be more credible than others. Those that are regarded highly credible (Doctor, Scientist, Educator, Judge) are held in high societal esteem while those regarded as non-credible (Lawyer, Politician, Used Car Salesman, Journalist) are sometimes reviled or denigrated.

As relates to the personal power augmented by The 4-C's, credibility is not dependent on another's opinion or perception. Rather it is a deliberate effort made by the empowered individual to always speak truth, constantly act with honesty and fairness, avoid hypocrisy like the plague, continuously display integrity and practice word as bond.

A competitor that brings credibility to the arena won't try to cheat to beat or deceive to win. Their credibility will precede them, their reputation will define them and if it's a close call as to who to believe the decision will probably be in their favor.

Those that would compete against a person with credibility will find it hard to trap her or him. Those who compete with it, will do so with the certainty that cheaters rarely win, and that honest, fair play will produce a champion to be emulated, celebrated and above all respected.

3. CREDENTIALS

Credentials are the paper that verifies (makes credible) the capabilities an individual has obtained. They are written documentation of accomplishment and achievement, or a tangible recognition of affiliation with certain groups. Most professions provide credentials as a form of group identification (Badges, I.D. and Business Cards, etc.) but as a component of The 4-C's, credentials refer to paper that indicates capability or qualifications: diplomas, degrees, certificates, occupational licenses, awards, commendations.

Many people possess capabilities for which they have no credentials (unlicensed plumber, barber, contractor), or skill-sets which require credentials before they can be included (commercial drivers, airline pilots, line and prep cooks). Credentials don't make an individual better than another who does not have them. What they do is increase options and choices because those with the ability to provide other people opportunity usually use credentials to help decide whom to give it to.

Because credentials come at a significant expenditure of both time and money, people seeking a short cut or desirous of working "under the radar" choose to try make it without them which, in the majority of cases is a mistake that hinders the ability to accomplish 'The Four Things'.

Credentials in the 21st century have become either an exclusionary or inclusionary device. Those that can use credentials to certify capability or accomplishment are often given high rungs on the workplace ladder while those that can't in many cases occupy the lower rungs. Most without credentials struggle to obtain and maintain but those that have them are more likely to sustain and attain.

4. CHARACTER

There are numerous and varied definitions of the word character in the English language but in relation to The 4-C's character refers to the essence of a person. Character seeks to define what type of individual someone is based on the qualities, traits and *character*istics a person displays.

Character is created and formed by a number of external and internal forces including mindset, perception, nurture and nature. A person's character is shaped (for good or bad) through life experience, education, parental influence, peer pressure and to a degree, the moral foundation an individual has built.

A person's character though self-developed, is generally appraised through the perception of other people. This assessment is a subjective evaluation, based on the value system of the people that are making the judgement.

Character, the essence of a person, adds to the unstoppable force of The 4-C's because of its close association with individual values which we discussed in chapter twelve. Character puts front and center and displays for all who care to look exactly who somebody else is and what they're all about.

An individual's character is the very manifestation of what principles the person holds, what steps they will take to win, which lines they will not cross. Knowing the character of the competitor will often provide a strategy to use and tactics to employ in order to win. In fact, knowing the character of others will indicate who you can possibly trust and whom should probably be avoided. Being capable of discerning the character of people in your circle will reduce the risk that they could trip you up or entrap you in their game.

Knowing your own character will allow the opportunity to select as associates only those whose character complements yours. It will give you the answer to the question of who you are and what you're about. Displaying your character will proclaim to the world that not only are you capable, credible and credentialed but that your actions and behavior are guided by the principles that you have chosen to embrace.

CHAPTER EIGHTEEN

ONE WORD TO DESCRIBE YOU

Frequently, when discussing the lifelong benefits offered by acquiring and displaying The 4-C's, my classroom starts to buzz with enthusiasm and cross-talk as the students begin to grasp how to use them to earn an advanced degree, get a better job, or move from their current situation to what they hope will be a life of satisfaction.

Nearing the end of the Program, most of them are at ease with me and each other. They've been on a six or seven week journey of discovery, with people that were once strangers but now had become intimate acquaintances. They'd traveled someplace together and as with most trips, as the destination came into view, camaraderie had been forged and excitement was heightened.

The group seems and acts profoundly different than when we first met. I can almost feel the growth they've experienced and often hear in their voices and see by their attitude that their confidence, self-esteem and awareness of life's possibilities has never been higher.

Feeling good about them and optimistic for their future opportunities I announce, "let's shift gears." As the room quiets down I ask my cohort, "give me one word to describe you." Uncertainty greets my unexpected question. "Think about it for a minute" I prod, "then we'll start with the first row and go quickly around the room. "Ready," I ask, pushing them into action.

"Determined" say's a voice. "Motivated" says another. "Hard working" one student responds, and I reply with a smile, "that's two words." The room fills with laughter as my students relax with the task then their answers begin to flow unbidden, one after another, in rapid fire.

> "Intelligent – Funny – Wise – Committed – Empowered –
> Successful – Energetic – Athletic Compassionate – Loving
> – Mother – Dedicated – Strong – Courageous – Driven
> – Friendly Trustworthy – Fearless – Sexy – Unique."

After the final response, the students silently review the adjectives I'd listed on the whiteboard seemingly stunned by the variety of the replies and the high self-worth each word conveyed. After a moment to absorb the content and see how each student perceived themselves I declare, "what you've just described is a trait, a characteristic of your personality that indicates your character."

Stepping up to the board and emphasizing each word by circling it with a green marker, I continue, "these words are extremely powerful in and of themselves. But what gives these words their *personal* power is that you have chosen them for yourselves. I didn't call any of you any of these words, you yourself did that. These words are *Self-Identifiers*, and as such they are powerful motivational tools because generally, what one self-identifies as, one usually tries to live up to."

Pausing a moment to let that thought sink in, I gather myself to deliver one of the main points of the day's lesson plan. "I notice no one said great, why not I wonder," my voice rising slightly at the end to indicate a puzzling question. I remained quiet, waiting so long for a response that the silence started to become uncomfortable. Finally after what seemed like minutes, a soft spoken student said in a hesitant voice, "It sounds like bragging to call myself great. It sounds arrogant."

I matched her low tone with one of my own. Looking directly into her eyes I asked, "don't you think you're great?" My student held my gaze for a moment then shook her head negatively and dropped her eyes. Taking a chance too good to pass up I queried the group one by one. "Do you think you're great"? A handful answered yes. The majority said no. One said he wasn't sure but that he wanted to be.

Realizing that this could be a pivotal moment to provide understanding and a crucial opportunity to add impact to my message of potential, I took my time then a deep breath and began by addressing the first comment made.

"I agree that it sounds arrogant to tell someone that you are great. It does sound like bragging, and as we all know from experience if you're ready to brag you better be ready to prove it, to back up your words with deeds.

But a *Self-Identifier* is exactly what it sounds like. You're not telling other people that you're great, you're telling *yourself*. You're using your *Self-Identifier* to motivate yourself into doing the actions that will back up what you tell yourself that you are.

You can lie to others, but you can't lie to yourself. It is impossible to believe in your greatness if you're not doing the things to bring it about, but it is entirely possible to do the things that will produce the identity you've claimed *if* you genuinely believe you are what you claim to be."

Widening my view to include all the students in the room, my pace increased like a racehorse sensing the finish line. "EVERY SINGLE ONE OF US IN THIS ROOM HAS THE POTENTIAL TO BE GREAT," I roared. "Potential is the ability or capacity available for use or development. Maximized potential simply means that our capacity, our individual ability to hold *and use* enormous amounts of wisdom, compassion, generosity, courage, talent and empathy has been developed and is available to help us realize, *to help us know* our greatness."

I could tell my students were engaged in what I was saying but I wasn't sure that they fully grasped what I was trying to let them know. Reaching for an analogy to help make or reinforce my point I advised, "think of potential like the sack used by Santa Claus.

Santa's magic sack has the capacity, the room, to carry toys and gifts for all the world's children, and the ability to hold those presents snugly and securely while being transported on the back of a flying sleigh. Santa's sack can expand at will to hold an abundance of joyful delights or shrink on demand to protect the few that remain as he nears the end of his Christmas Eve deliveries.

Human potential is just as magical as Santa Claus' sack. It can easily expand as individuals Max-Their-Po in an attempt to realize their greatness. It can also easily contract or shrink from disuse when the effort to increase greatness falters. Sometimes, for people who aren't empowered, potential never gets it's chance to magically expand. It remains in a shrunken state like a forgotten Christmas orange that was stored out of sight."

Nobody said anything after I'd finished my analogy. Then a hand raised in the back and one of my male students asked, "so, Mr. Miller, what's your *Self-Identifier*?" I shot him a mischievous grin and replied with an incredulous tone, "what, you want me to give away *all* of my secrets?"

CHAPTER NINETEEN

THE POWER IS INSIDE YOU

I gave a flippant answer to the young man's question primarily because I wanted to preserve the aura of mystery and unpredictability many teachers use to engage their students while maintaining personal distance. I wanted my cohort to focus on the material rather than the instructor.

On top of that, I couldn't quickly recall what *Self-Identifier* I was using at his age. I knew when I was young that I wanted to be great, but I didn't know if that would be possible; everybody back then was telling me to "remember my place, keep my head down, don't be an agitator and don't make waves."

Reflecting on his question later that night, I realized that more than anything else when I was young, I thought of myself as courageous and bold. I carried those strong words as my *Self-Identifiers* throughout my teen's and into early adulthood. I had my share of mis-steps, tasted failure and success, went where I chose to go and played with a relentless spirit to get what I thought was my due.

I came to know what I'm sharing with you in these pages through years of study and work, decades of experience and an expanded awareness of what is possible as I learned about people, their diverse cultures and, despite what the dividers may tell us, our many similarities and commonalities.

I didn't tell my young man any of this because I didn't want to take valuable class time to get into a "side bar" conversation about my upbringing and also because the empowerment classes I teach aren't about me, nor is this book. This book is about you. It's about the awesome power that lies inside you waiting to be harnessed. It's about how to summon that power, at will, and use it to fulfill your needs and desires.

It's not that difficult to see the big picture when all the pieces of the puzzle come together; the big picture called success. As discussed in chapter eleven, our cultural notion of success is tremendously misguided. To many, success is quantified by how much excess a person displays on the outside, how much a person owns or is worth financially.

Rarely is success touted for what it should be measured as, what a person does to influence the thoughts actions and ideas of other people, or what someone does to produce positive change. Despite what the dictionary says success is more verb than noun. Success is what you do, not what you own.

The power to do is in you right now and will remain inside you, God willing, for the duration of your journey here. Mindset triggers the will to do and determines when and how to do it. As long as we refuse to have our mindset co-opted or cede control of it to an outside source or influence, success will always be attainable.

In the United States, those classified as citizens are fortunate to have the freedom (despite ageism, racism, sexism, Trumpism and the rest of the schisms that get in the way) to dream. We're lucky to have the opportunity to try to make those dreams real; to go for the gold, strive for the top, and find the pot filled with satisfaction at the end of the rainbow.

Unlike other countries and nation states with oppressive and restrictive systems, where the government or dictator or oligarchs control everything including information, speech, thought and upward mobility, Americans are free to open their minds, their mouths and go where they please.

In contrast to repressive regimes that stifle individual achievement, restrict financial opportunity, limit education options and deny economic prosperity to the majority of the people, we're allowed to earn our own way, invest for our future, operate businesses, create products, develop innovations and vote to try to protect our interests. We're able in fact, to learn all we can and do all we will to shape our individual existence and that of our community.

In short, despite the coronavirus pandemic, racial injustice protests, gridlock in our politics and glaring societal inequities, we Americans are in the perfect spot to maximize our potential. We're living at the perfect time to showcase our brilliance to not only find the way out of the darkness of these times, but to shine a spotlight on the best path forward.

The chaos of our present time finds many of our fellow citizens clamoring for more aid, more assistance, more help in dealing with the fallout from the ravages of COVID-19, climate change, police brutality and a burgeoning mental illness epidemic.

Some of us need rent relief while landlords need to be paid. Thousands grapple with utility shutoffs and foreclosure. Millions are still laid off. Businesses have failed. Tax revenue is down. Infrastructure is crumbling. Mass shooters continue their carnage. Hunger is a daily occurrence for far too many of us while homelessness and domestic violence are trending up in alarming numbers.

Above all death, loss and grief have seemed ever present and the despair from the personal devastation caused by the virus, climate disasters, gun violence and ethnic hatred have left many of us reeling, which is why the clamor for help is so deafeningly loud.

As is often the case when one is bombarded by non-stop uproar, it becomes hard to think clearly and difficult to discern what is noise versus what is real.

So let me drown out the clatter. ***The power inside you is real***. The steps to take to get to where you want to go have been detailed in these pages, but your power can only be activated by you. Once activated only you can maintain it. Only you can control it to drive you to your destiny.

I titled this book, *'The Power's Inside'* as a play on the word powers. The apostrophe 's substitutes for the word *is* to reveal that the power is already inside us. The awesome, magical powers of potential that when maximized will increase momentum, create opportunity, provide personal fulfilment, and lead to a lifetime of success for you and those you love.

The predominant media messages of our present era, *'to get the life you deserve, and get it fast, easy or free'*, is part of the noise that drowns out the truth. Without question, all of us deserve respect, opportunity and fairness but beyond that it's up to the individual to obtain the things they need and want. It falls on the individual to maintain and sustain those things. Success or failure is an *individual* thing because success is what *you* do.

What the message should be is that *failure* comes fast, easy and free but success takes time, hard work and comes at a price. Society always puts up barriers to achievement, which is what helps to keep the status quo in place. Overcoming obstacles and breaking through barriers, especially those maintained by people who would limit the competition, is time consuming, difficult and costly.

For those of you like me, who refuse to be blocked from your chances to succeed, power is required to go over, under, around or through the things or people that would keep you out of the game. Personal power that is activated by your curiosity. Personal power ignited by your empowered mindset. Personal power fueled by your maximized potential and driven by your self-actualized dreams.

The power to win when you compete waits inside you. The power is in you now to determine your values, embrace them and keep them close. You hold the power to build relationships to rely on and to choose trustworthy people to include in your circle. The power of *Super-Literacy* is yours to absorb. The power of effective communication is yours to acquire and use.

You possess the power to control your fear; the power to replace fearfulness with courage in any attempt to *Max-Yo-Po*. The power's inside to resolve conflict, avoid the traps, or if you can't, to get out of them. The power to be self-sufficient, to be confident, to be respected, to have influence, and to succeed throughout every step of your journey is inside you as you read this.

The four elements to maximized potential, mindset, behavior, action steps and individual planning are critical to your power activation but what you do is of utmost importance to your success. To decide what to do, what actions to take, *The Sixteen 'P's to Potential* (chapter 11) provide the template.

However, to increase the likelihood that you are doing the things that will provide a life of enjoyment, contentment, happiness and satisfaction it is imperative that you discover your God-given purpose and find your God-given talent. If you've yet to discover your purpose, that's all right, work your talent until you do because talent is often indicative of purpose.

Our country and the communities that connect us to each other need powerful people more now than perhaps at any time in our history. Finding and implementing solutions to climate change, food distribution, infrastructure repair, poverty, homelessness, systemic racism, pervasive violence, misinformation, mental illness and the fear of our fellows, is too big a job to leave to the politicians, elected officials, big business, or the clergy.

When I came of age, "power to the people" was a rallying cry bellowed by all who agitated for inclusion, equity and fairness. It was a tacit admission that we the people had allowed others with interests in conflict to our own to control our individual destinies. What was true then remains true today, most don't give up their power or share it with agitators. Instead they impose additional barriers to keep the protestors at bay or offer a morsel of change in hopes of pacifying those whose demands they refuse to meet.

Now, as we enter the third decade of the 21st century a majority of the American populace still looks to the so called "leaders" to blaze the trail and set the course. They look *outside* rather than *inside* to help them personally obtain, maintain, sustain and attain.

They're looking in the wrong place because the power's inside. When you decide to commit to your own power, use this book as your guide.

AFTERWORD

I began this work in the waning days of 2020, just before the United States National election. In the nine months that have passed since then a whirlwind of events have gripped our National consciousness and shaken our country to its core.

The refusal of the "former guy" to concede his loss to Joe Biden in the Presidential contest, while fueling animosity, division and fear through non-stop lies that the election was stolen, and the entire process was fraudulent.

The worthless effort by Donald Trump and his minions to reverse the ballot box decision through legal challenges, intimidation, bullying, mendacity and the perverse willingness to destroy what they could not hold onto or burn it down on the way out of town.

The stupidly dangerous attempt to overturn majority rule, replace it with mob rule, and disrupt the peaceful transfer of power from one Administration to the next by mal-contents, conspiracy nuts and white supremacist losers. A transition that had, before January 6, 2021, never been in doubt or in question.

The House of Representatives second impeachment of Trump for inciting a riot, fomenting insurrection and trying to steal the Election *himself* through an ill-concealed effort to stage a coup against his government, and thwart the will of the people who danced in the streets when they learned of his defeat. As expected, the Republican controlled Senate acquitted the former President of the impeachment charge thereby allowing him a chance to further influence events and attempt to shape policy.

The Republican Party leadership's spineless display of fealty to the would be usurper, and their in your face, "gas lighting", to minimize the damage caused by the failed rebellion at the Capitol building and absolve Trump of responsibility or culpability in his supporters attack on our Nation's traditions and our Democracy.

The incredible gullibility of the majority of Republican voters who refuse to see the dangerous rot that is in plain sight and have willingly embraced the lies told by the Republican status quo in a futile effort to maintain the existing order of things that will (they hope) keep them on top.

Two new Senators from Georgia, both Democrats elected in runoffs, shifted the balance of power in the U.S. Senate to a 50-50 split, giving a slight majority to the Democratic Party when the vote of the Vice President, Kamala Harris, is added.

The victories of Biden, Harris and the Democrats from Georgia, combined with the so called *"Big Lie"* of widespread election fraud prompted a backlash by several Republican led States, which resulted in a madcap rush to establish new legislation to restrict voter opportunities and limit Democratic turnout.

Meanwhile, to stop the financial hemorrhaging I spoke of in chapter one, President Biden took advantage of the Senate majority to pass the *'American Rescue Plan'*, a 1.9 trillion dollar package that will send boatloads of cash to states, cities and localities to help stabilize budgets and "build back better". The Feds are also sending big bucks to individuals, families, small businesses, schools, hospitals, nursing homes, airlines and travel industry components like cruise companies, hotels, passenger trains and entertainment venues.

This financial windfall, deemed urgent and necessary to our national recovery from the ravages of the coronavirus pandemic, comes at an extremely high cost because it is being paid for with borrowed money. In fact the U.S. Government expects to borrow 2.28 trillion dollars in fiscal year 2021 which, according to economists, will raise the total U.S financial deficit to a whopping 3.3 trillion dollars; the highest deficit in the history of the Country and a tremendous financial hole to climb out of!

On the social front, Derek Chauvin was convicted on all counts for the caught on tape murder of George Floyd and ultimately received a twenty-two and a half year sentence. Chauvin's guilty verdict, viewed in some circles as vindication for the systemic abuse of Black Americans at the hands of law enforcement, was barely entered into the books before additional accounts of police brutality and law enforcement over-reaction surfaced in multiple U.S. cities.

Gun violence has surged like a mini pandemic as the NRA's request for bankruptcy protection in Texas was denied. Physical attacks on Asian individuals have proliferated. Road rage and domestic violence occur with regularity. Ransomware cyberattacks illustrate the weakness of our infrastructure grid.

Joe Biden's administration delivered on his promise to vaccinate the nation in record time. Although many vaccine sceptics still choose to refuse their shot despite the stunning efficacy of the Moderna, Johnson and Johnson and Pfizer-BioNTech vaccines in blocking the virus, the speed in which the inoculations were carried out resulted in the cancellation of the nation-wide mask mandate and began our collective journey to the *new normal*.

However, the 2021 summer surge of coronavirus infections fueled by the delta variant of COVID-19, combined with the revelation that vaccinated people can become infected and pass the virus to others, indicates that a return to *normality* could be a long time coming.

Perhaps even more alarming though than the proliferation of the delta variant, is the second major reveal of the summer of '21; climate change is indisputably real. Record setting drought, record setting heat, record setting floods caused by record setting rains. Record setting infernos devouring record setting acres exposed the impact of global warming, and portends that *normal*, new or otherwise, could be gone forever.

While all of this was going on in America, most of the world's population was also in turmoil. No matter where one looked it seemed as if many of the world's governments have gone to war against their own people. In Hong Kong, Myanmar, Russia and Turkey, Ethiopia, Brazil, Israel and Iraq; government pushback on citizens intent on forcing change and controlling their own destiny have grown ever more repressive, perilous and deadly.

Brexit's enactment in the United Kingdom upended the financial structure and stability of Europe as the pandemic raged. Citizens from Africa, Asia, South America and numerous other regions of the globe became displaced refugees at the whim of despots; forced to flee their homelands for a new way of life in a different world.

Lurking unseen through the happenings of the past nine months was the coronavirus *Monster of Dread*, which will probably haunt and stalk us all for a generation or more. This monster has shown a mirror to the world's people. It has exposed us in ways both ugly and beautiful; the hoarding and disregard for others on the one hand, the sharing, compassion and willingness to assist on the other. The sheer brilliance of vaccine development, the misinformation about their effectiveness and the massive inequality in their distribution.

Now, less than a year after I started writing 'The Power's Inside', I marvel at all that has occurred in that short span of time and wonder what the next six, twelve or eighteen months will bring. I admit that in my uncertainty lies a sense of nervous anticipation, tinged with optimism and excitement.

Without a doubt you and I are living through a critical juncture, a time of great upheaval. We have the chance to shape the future for all who come after us. What we do now, for good or bad, will have ramifications that ripple through the millennia.

To do the right things in the right way demands an empowered citizenry and a super-literate society that is open to new ideas. It requires shared societal values and the ability to trust each other.

To shape the future for ourselves, our children and theirs will take maximum power. We'll need people power, financial power, industrial power and technological power. Most of all though, the ability to transform your world will depend on developing and unleashing the power inside you.

COMPILATION OF KEY CONCEPTS WITHIN 'THE POWER'S INSIDE'

Personal Empowerment (*Chapter 2*)

The knowledge and ability to remove or overcome any obstacle or impediment that blocks the acquisition of individual achievement.

Self-Actualization (*Chapter 2*)

Acquiring the drive, determination, motivation and skill-set to realize your full potential through action.

Four Elements to Maximize Potential (*Chapter 2*)

Mindset, Behavior, Action Steps, Individual Planning

Four Things Almost Everybody on the Planet is Trying to Do (*Chapter 3*)

Obtain, Maintain, Sustain, Attain

The Empowerment Principles (*Chapter 4*)

1. Super-Literacy Is Job #1
2. Knowing Where You Came From

3. Knowing Where You're Headed

4. Knowing How To Handle Yourself

5. Knowing How To Communicate

6. Having Options And Choices

7. Not Being Fearful

8. Not Being Victimized

9. Not Looking Over Your Shoulder

10. Cleaning Up Tickets, Debts & Financial Obligations

11. Being Able To Give To Others

12. Being Able To Turn On Your Own Ignition

Key Pieces to Complete Your Life's Puzzle (*Chapter 7*)

Curiosity, Talent, Big Dreams, Purpose

The Twin Traps (*Chapter 9*)

Fear & Ignorance

The Winning Combination (*Chapter 10*)

What You Know, What You Do, What You Are

Sixteen 'P's to Success (*Chapter 11*)

Purpose, Plan, Prioritize, Prepare, Participate, Practice, Pride, Perform, Prayer, Persistence, Perseverance, Perception, Principled, Punctuality, Positive Personality, Patience

The Winning Values (*Chapter 12*)

Integrity, Honesty, Loyalty, Sharing, Thrift, Mentoring, Education, Family First, Punctuality,

Forgiveness, Cleanliness, Responsibility, Super-Literacy, Industriousness, Word As Bond, Healthy Habits, Higher Power, The Golden Rule, Entrepreneurship, Honor Commitments, Fair Play.

The Power Equation (*Chapter 13*)

No Trust Equals No Unity. No Unity Equals No Strength. No Strength Equals No Protection. No Protection Equals No Power.

The 3 C's of Conflict Resolution (*Chapter 14*)

Communication, Consensus, Compromise

The Seven Point Action Plan (*Chapter 16*)

1. Objective
2. Timeline
3. Research
4. Prioritize
5. Action Steps
6. Daily To-Do Lists
7. Review, Revise, Refine

The 4 C's That Produce an Unstoppable Force (*Chapter 17*)

1. Capability
2. Credibility
3. Credentials
4. Character

A LITTLE BIT
ABOUT THE AUTHOR

Media entrepreneur, broadcast journalist, educator and motivator, Jeffrey Miller has long been involved in the business of changing public perception. In 1989 Mr. Miller left a successful sales career in Corporate America to augment the process of balancing mainstream media's portrayal of the Black experience.

In 1990, he launched the Media Company, Jammin II Incorporated, which became a trendsetter in Black issues programming, and a heavy hitter in the struggle for full inclusion of "people of color" as valued U.S. citizens.

As the company's CEO, Jeffrey Miller also performed as the Executive Producer, Principal Writer and Host of Jammin II Inc.'s video projects and was engaged for more than sixteen years in the creation and distribution of groundbreaking television, including weekly TV series', documentaries and 'Special Reports'.

His productions earned two Broadcast Emmys, two CABLEACE Awards and eleven nominations for Outstanding Programming Achievement from the National Academy of Arts & Sciences, and the National Cable Association.

In 2008 Mr. Miller wrote, published and secured distribution for, *'Up From the Under, What We Should Do Next'*. This mind opening audio-book weaves a fascinating historical story, with a contemporary blend of events. It also presents a step by step blueprint to follow for a Generation seeking the way up from 'the under', as in, under-educated, under-employed, under-paid, under-privileged, under-valued, under-housed, under-suspicion and often under attack.

For the past thirteen years, Jeff Miller has worked with state of Michigan agencies, Detroit based community groups, churches, schools and non-profits to develop and implement a Personal Enrichment Program Series designed to *inspire, motivate and actualize individual success.* He designed and continues to facilitate a Self-Actualization and Personal Empowerment curriculum, created to change the mindset of failure and alter the culture of ignorance that leads to 'the under'.

His Program, **'The Empowerment Project with Jeffrey Miller'**, is about personal uplift through knowledge. It's about becoming competent, capable and confident. It's about handling conflict, communicating effectively, building healthy relationships, competing, winning, and learning how to maximize individual potential to supersize success.

Now with *'The Power's Inside'*, Jeff hopes to share his transformative message with all those that seek control of their destiny but are unsure how to make that happen or are doubtful of their ability to thrive.